THE COMPLETE HIGH-PROTEIN MEAL PREP GUIDE & COOKBOOK

6-Week Meal Plan with Easy & Delicious, High-Protein Meals for Muscle Gain, Weight Loss & Getting Lean | UK metric measurements

Simon Alex Martin

Copyright ©2024 by Simon Alex Martin. All rights reserved.
THE COMPLETE HIGH-PROTEIN MEAL PREP GUIDE & COOKBOOK

No part of this publication may be reproduced, distributed or transmitted in any form or by any means, including photocopying, recording or other electronic or mechanical methods, without the prior written permission of the publisher, except in the case of brief quotations embodied in critical reviews and certain other non-commercial uses permitted by copyright law.

TABLE OF CONTENTS

INTRODUCTION 5

CHAPTER 1: THE POWER OF MEAL PREP 7
- What are the benefits of meal prep? 7
- Meal prep practicalities before getting started 8

CHAPTER 2: MACRONUTRIENTS, A BREAKDOWN OF THE BIG 3 10
- Proteins: The Building Blocks of MuscleError! Bookmark not defined. 10
- Carbohydrates: The body's energizing torch 13
- Fats: The essential players 15

CHAPTER 3: MICRONUTRIENTS, THE POWERHOUSE PLAYERS 17

CHAPTER 4: TIPS FROM CHAMPIONS & TROUBLE SHOOTING 19
- Champion Routines and Mindset for unwavering motivation 19
- Pre and post workout nutrition 22
- Rest and Recovery 22
- Clean eating, cheating and dealing with cravings 24
- Meditation for body and mind 26

CHAPTER 5: INDIVIDUAL MACRO SPLIT AND PORTION CONTROL 27
- BMR: The Engine's Idle – What it is and why it matters 27
- TDEE: The Real-world fuel gauge, unveiling your daily needs 28
- How do you choose the right macros split? 29
- How do you adapt a recipe to your selected macros split? 32
- Once you have selected a macro split, when should you change it? 34

CHAPTER 6: RECIPES, MEAL PLANNING AND PREPPING 36
- Schedule meal prep Week 1 38
- Grocery list week 1 39
- Turkey with veggies and whole wheat pita wraps 40
- Salmon with asparagus, cucumber, cherry tomatoes and brown rice 41
- Grilled chicken skewers with veggies and brown rice 42
- Classic roast beef with crispy roasties 43
- Meal prep step by step instructions week 1 44
- Schedule meal prep Week 2 46
- Grocery list week 2 47
- Pork meatballs with quinoa salad 48
- Beef and bean chili 49
- Roast chicken with roasted potatoes 50
- Salmon, courgette and quinoa salad 51
- Meal prep step by step instructions week 2 52
- Schedule meal prep Week 3 54
- Grocery list week 3 55
- Tuna and avocado salad with Basmati rice 56
- Chicken and Veg Stir-Fry with Noodles 57
- Bangers and mashed potatoes 58
- Beef, broccoli and basmati rice 59

Meal prep step by step instructions week 3	60
Schedule meal prep Week 4	61
Grocery list week 4	62
Spicy chicken with couscous	63
Salmon with veg and whole wheat pasta	64
Pesto chicken with roasted broccoli and cauliflower	65
Vegetarian chickpea, couscous and spinach curry	66
Meal prep step by step instructions week 4	67
Schedule meal prep Week 5	69
Grocery list week 5	70
Beef burrito bowl with brown rice	71
Feta cheese and roasted tomato couscous	72
Lentils & couscous stuffed bell peppers	73
Chicken and brown rice casserole	74
Meal prep step by step instructions week 5	75
Schedule meal prep Week 6	77
Grocery list week 6	78
Prawn, courgette and rice stir-fry	79
Cottage cheese, green beans and quinoa salad	80
Beef burgers and sweet potato wedges	81
Grilled turkey breast with lemon herb rice	82
Meal prep step by step instructions week 6	83
Super speedy breakfasts (5 mins max & balanced high protein macros)	85
Double decker smoky salmon and cottage cheese on rye bread	86
Smashed avocado with poached egg on toast	87
Stovetop scrambled eggs with berries	88
Fruity yoghurt bowl	89
Nut butter and banana on toast	90
Berry oats with nut butter	91
BONUS	**92**
CONVERSION TABLE	**93**
INDEX	**94**
CONCLUSION	**95**

INTRODUCTION

Building a fit, lean and healthy body is not just about lifting weights or throwing yourself at intense gym workouts. The right food fuels muscle growth, aids repair and optimises your performance. Nutrition is the foundation of your journey, regardless of your goal: cutting to shed body fat while building muscle definition for a lean and toned physique, bulking to gain muscle mass or maintaining to preserve your existing muscle mass.

Here is the truth though: without dedicated effort towards nutrition, your gym sessions will not be enough to achieve your dream physique. For many of us however, fitting in consistent, healthy meals amidst a busy week can feel like a daunting task. That's where meal planning and prepping come to the rescue!

Meal planning and meal preparation (*meal prep*) go hand-in-hand. Meal planning involves deciding what meals you will eat throughout the week and meal prep means cooking them in one sitting. With just a couple of hours of preparation and cooking once a week, you will have delicious and nutritious meals ready to grab and go for the whole following week.

Whether you are a complete beginner or a seasoned athlete, this book is your guide to effortless and efficient meal prep: no more frantically searching for unhealthy last-minute meals or wondering what to cook and how to ensure your meals hit your individual macro and calorie goals.

When I first embarked on my fitness journey, I soon realised that opening the fridge meant for me a continuous battle against indecision, resulting in meals that were not always aligned with the right macros. That is where the real journey began – my venture into the world of meal prep.

Those early days were not exactly kitchen triumphs. I spent long hours in the kitchen on a series of culinary experiments, trying out various recipes, facing the same challenges you might be encountering right now. Initially the idea of planning and prepping many meals beforehand felt overwhelming. However here is the thing: I knew the importance of a structured meal plan prepared in advance.

Through a combination of cooking experimentation and recipe remixes along with meticulous research, I have designed an easy-to-follow high-protein meal prep plan with step-by-step instructions to support any fitness goal. The core principles of portion control, personalised macronutrient intake and meal planning & prepping apply to everyone. You can easily adapt the recipes included in the 6-week meal plan to fuel your own fitness journey, whatever your goal is.

Before we dive into the recipes and practical meal prep plan, let's break down the science behind food including micro & macronutrients and learn how a high-protein diet can be beneficial. Knowing why these nutrients are essential for your body empowers you to make informed choices and fuels your journey to success. Finally, this book will provide guidance on choosing the right individual macronutrient split and show you how to adapt the recipes to your own needs.

Simon Alex Martin

Chapter 1: The power of Meal Prep

What are the benefits of meal prep?

Time is money (and muscle): We all face the same challenge – balancing work, training, family commitments, social life and somehow finding time to cook healthy meals in the right macros every single day. Meal prep is your time-saving weapon. Invest one to two hours on a weekend and you will be rewarded with stress-free, healthy meals for the whole workweek. No more scrambling after work, no more unhealthy choices born out of desperation. Just grab, heat and go – conquer your day, conquer your goals!

Portion control, your key to achieving your physique goals: Let's face it, eyeballing portions are not always the most accurate science. Meal prep takes the guesswork out of portion control. You will be dishing up perfectly measured meals, ensuring you are hitting your macros and staying on track. No more overindulging or under-fuelling, just the right amount of protein, carbs and healthy fats to build your dream healthy physique. Consistency is key and meal prep provides the perfect platform to achieve it.

Say goodbye to diet sabotage: Meal prep removes temptation and cravings from the equation. When your healthy meals are readily available, the greasy takeaway loses its appeal. Plus, let's be honest, wouldn't you rather be opening a Tupperware filled with your masterpiece creation than a cardboard box filled with questionable ingredients?

Efficient budget: Meal prep allows you to plan your meals around your budget. No more impulse buys at the supermarket, no more expensive convenience meals. You will be buying ingredients in bulk (saving you cash!) and ensuring minimal food waste. Every penny counts when you're building muscle and meal prep ensures your hard-earned money goes towards the good stuff – quality ingredients that fuel your body.

So, are you ready to take control of your meals, your time and your physique? Meal prep is your key to unlocking a world of fitness success. Turn the page and let's embark on this delicious journey together. I will guide you through the meal prep process step-by-step, from choosing the right containers to creating simple mouthwatering recipes in the right personalised macros that will tantalize your taste buds and power your goals!

Meal prep practicalities before getting started

Let's go quickly through the basic kitchen equipment required before cooking. Before you head out and buy anything new, I suggest you take a quick look of your existing kitchen equipment.

Choose the right airtight containers: For your meal prep lunch and dinner meals aim for containers around 800ml. You can either buy glass or plastic containers. Glass containers are often microwave-safe while plastic containers might require transferring your food to a microwave-safe dish first. It's always wise to double-check the label for microwave safety before use. Alternatively,  you can reheat your meals on the stovetop for more even heating. However, glass can be heavier, take more space and potentially break if dropped. Plastic containers are lightweight, durable and can come in a variety of sizes and colours. The best choice for you ultimately between glass and plastic containers depends on your preferences. Whatever you choose between plastic or glass, look for containers with secure lids that have a good seal to prevent leaks. A tight seal of course prevents food spoilage, it creates a barrier between your food and the outside world, preventing air and moisture from getting in. This not only keeps your meals fresher for longer but also prevents any unwanted odours from invading your fridge. Most high-quality airtight containers can be used for both fridge and freezer storage. Please note that the middle shelves of your fridge are usually the coolest zone, perfect for storing meals you plan to consume within 3 days. Stack your containers neatly, ensuring they are labelled with the date and contents for easy identification.

Essential utensils and cooking equipment: Let's go quickly through the basic kitchen equipment required before cooking. Before you head out and buy anything new, I suggest you take a quick look of your existing kitchen equipment.

 Sharp chef's knife, ideal for chopping vegetables, meat and anything else that needs a good dice.

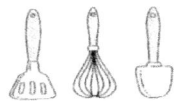 Serving/Mixing Spoon (spatula), for flipping meat, transferring ingredients and general mixing.

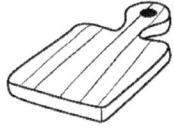 Chopping board, essential for chopping. Consider having two boards, one for raw meat and fish and another for vegetables, to prevent cross-contamination.

 Food scale, for accurate portion control of ingredients.

 Large frying pan, perfect for searing meat and grilling and another smaller frying pan for frying eggs or heating up breakfast components.

 Large saucepan, for simmering chili, boiling grains and other cooking needs.

 Baking tray and a roasting tin, essential for roasting vegetables, potatoes and some protein options.

 Mixing bowls, you will likely need a couple of bowls for mixing ingredients, marinades and preparing sauces.

Grocery shopping. While most ingredients for your meal prep can be found at your local supermarket, consider exploring farmers' markets for fresh, seasonal produce. Here in the UK, we are fortunate to have access to a wide variety of high-quality ingredients. "Bio" food, also known as organic food, is produced without the use of synthetic pesticides or fertilisers. While organic options can be a healthy choice, they might be slightly more expensive. The most important factor is to choose fresh, high-quality ingredients that fit your budget and dietary needs. Don't be intimidated by fancy gadgets or expensive ingredients. Again, focus on practicality, quality and choosing foods that align with your goals and budget.
Last but not least, invest in a roll of food labels and a permanent marker. Labelling your prepped meals with the date and contents is important for organisation and safety.

Chapter 2: Macronutrients, a breakdown of the big 3

The three macronutrients' carbohydrates, proteins and fats provide the building blocks and energy to fuel yourself. Now let's delve into the fascinating world of macronutrients, exploring their roles, functions, benefits and how to optimize their intake for your goals.

Proteins: The Building Blocks of MuscleError! Bookmark not defined.

Protein is the undisputed king of muscle building. It's composed of amino acids, the very building blocks your body uses to repair, rebuild and grow muscle tissue. It is important to acknowledge that protein's significance extends far beyond the realm of muscles. It plays a vital role in the health and function of numerous tissues throughout your body. As a matter of fact, protein acts as the structural scaffolding for many tissues, including your skin, hair and nails. A consistent intake of protein ensures these tissues remain strong and healthy.

Why should you aim for a high-protein diet? What are the benefits?

Boosting metabolism: Protein digestion requires more energy compared to other macronutrients. This translates to a slight increase in your metabolic rate, meaning your body burns more calories at rest. A high-protein diet impacts on your metabolic rate, through a scientific phenomenon known as thermic effect of food (TEF). TEF represents the energy your body expends to digest, absorb and utilize nutrients from your food. Different macronutrients (carbohydrates, protein and fat) have varying TEF values. Protein boasts the highest TEF, meaning your body burns more calories simply processing it compared to carbohydrates or fats. Muscle tissue plays a significant role in your resting metabolic rate (RMR) – the number of calories your body burns at rest. Muscle is metabolically active, constantly burning calories even when you're not actively exercising. However, during periods of calorie restriction or low protein intake, your body may resort to breaking down muscle tissue for energy. This process, known as muscle catabolism, not only weakens your muscles but also reduces your RMR, making it harder to burn calories overall.

Here's where protein shines. A high-protein diet helps preserve muscle mass, which in turn, helps maintain a higher RMR. This translates to a more efficient metabolism, even when you're at rest, allowing you to burn more calories throughout the day.

Faster recovery following exercise: By strategically increasing your protein intake, you're providing your muscles with the necessary resources to facilitate faster recovery after your workouts, leading to improved performance and muscle growth. After a challenging workout, protein helps your muscles recover from microscopic tears, promoting muscle growth and strength development. Consuming adequate protein, especially post-workout, it provides the amino acids your muscles need to repair and grow. This enhanced recovery translates to a heightened capacity for muscle repair and adaptation, leading to improved performance and ultimately, the achievement of your fitness goals. Faster recovery after exercise leads to improved performance and muscle growth

Satiety saviour and appetite control: Protein keeps you feeling fuller for longer, reducing cravings and aiding in appetite control. This can be particularly beneficial during calorie restriction phases when managing your overall calorie intake is crucial. Feeling satisfied helps you stay on track. Protein's influence extends beyond simply feeling full after a meal. It regulates the release of hormones like ghrelin, often referred to as the "hunger hormone," which bombards your brain with cravings. By promoting the release of peptide YY (PYY), a satiety hormone, protein effectively silences these hunger pangs. Additionally, protein's complex structure requires a longer digestion process compared to carbohydrates or fats. This translates to a sustained feeling of fullness, ensuring you're not left reaching for unhealthy snacks between meals. This isn't just about short-term cravings; it's about harnessing the power of protein to fuel your body efficiently and support your long-term health goals.

Muscle preservation and ageing: As we get older, we all experience a natural decline in muscle mass, a condition known as sarcopenia. This can lead to decreased strength, balance issues, and a higher risk of falls. Protein is essential for muscle growth and repair. By incorporating a high-protein diet into your routine, you're providing your body with the ammunition it needs to maintain muscle mass and strength, even as you age. This translates to better mobility, improved balance, and a reduced risk of injuries. Think of it as investing in your future – a high-protein diet can help you stay active and independent for longer.

Stronger bones: Not only muscles! Our bones are a living tissue constantly undergoing renewal. Protein is a vital building block for collagen, the major protein component in bones. Think of collagen as the scaffolding that provides structure and strength to your bones. By ensuring adequate protein intake, you're essentially supplying the raw materials your body needs to maintain strong, healthy bones. This becomes even more important as we age, as bone density naturally starts to decline. A high-protein diet can help combat this decline, reducing the risk of osteoporosis, a condition characterized by weak and brittle bones.

A strong immune system defence: Antibodies, the foot soldiers of your immune system, are primarily composed of protein. Ensuring adequate protein intake helps support a robust immune system, better equipped to fight off illness and infection. In simpler terms, adequate protein intake acts as a strategic investment in your body's natural defences, helping you stay healthy and resilient in the face of potential illness. The antibodies are molecules crafted primarily from protein and act as highly specific recognition units, binding to and neutralising pathogens like bacteria and viruses.

Safe protein intake: How much do you need?

Determining your optimal protein intake is not a one-size-fits-all equation. It depends on various factors like your age, activity level and overall health goals. Current research suggests a daily protein target ranging from 0.8 to 1.6 grams per kilogram of body weight. This translates to a macronutrient ratio where protein sits comfortably between 30% and 40% of your daily calorie intake. The remaining calories can be distributed strategically between carbohydrates and healthy fats. Please jump to chapter 5 of this book to calculate your own personalised individual needs.

Let's now see what the main protein sources are. Remember variety is key. By incorporating a diverse range of protein-rich options into your meals, you will be well on your way to supplying your body with the building blocks it needs to achieve your goals.

Animal proteins
Lean Meats: Chicken breast, fish, and turkey are all excellent sources of complete protein, meaning they contain all nine essential amino acids your body needs.
Eggs: A true bodybuilding staple, whole eggs and egg whites offer high-quality protein in a convenient package.

Dairy delights
Greek Yogurt: This protein-packed yogurt is a delicious post-workout snack or can be incorporated into smoothies for a satisfying protein boost.
Cottage Cheese: A classic for bodybuilders, cottage cheese provides a slow-digesting protein source, perfect for sustained muscle recovery.

Plant-based proteins
Beans and Lentils: Don't underestimate the power of plants. Beans and lentils are excellent sources of protein and fibre for everyone especially for vegetarians and vegans.
Tofu and Tempeh: These soy-based options offer a complete protein source for plant-based athletes, making them versatile additions to your diet.

Protein supplements
Whey Protein: A fast-digesting protein powder, whey protein is a popular choice for post-workout shakes, providing a rapid infusion of amino acids to aid muscle repair and growth.
Casein Protein: A slower-digesting protein, casein can be a valuable addition before bed or between meals, offering a sustained release of amino acids for ongoing muscle recovery.

Remember protein is crucial but is not a solo player and does not function in isolation. A balanced high-protein diet that includes sufficient carbohydrates and healthy fats alongside protein is essential for achieving your fitness goals. Think of it as a well-rounded team working together; protein providing the building blocks, carbs supplying energy and healthy fats supporting overall health and hormone function. By incorporating all three macronutrients in appropriate proportions, you can create the optimal environment for your goals.

Carbohydrates: The body's energizing torch

Imagine carbohydrates (carbs) as the quick-burning logs fuelling your metabolic fire. They break down into glucose, a readily absorbed sugar that your muscles readily consume during intense workouts and daily activities. However not all carbs are created equally.

There are two main types of carbohydrates, simple carbs (sugars) vs complex carbs (starches and fibre).

Simple carbs, the sugary treats like candy and white bread, cause blood sugar to spike and crash. While not entirely forbidden, these sugary snacks offer little sustained energy compared to their complex counterparts. This blood sugar crash can have a significant impact on your fitness journey. Consuming a sugary beverage or a sweet confectionary product prior  to exercise may induce a rapid rise in blood sugar levels, mimicking a surge of readily available energy. In response to the significant increase in blood sugar, the pancreas releases a large amount of insulin. While this is effective in lowering blood sugar levels, it can sometimes be too effective. The large amount of insulin released can usher too much glucose into the cells too quickly, leading to a rapid decline in blood sugar levels. This drop in blood sugar is what we call the "glycaemic dip" or "reactive hypoglycaemia." The initial rise in blood sugar, followed by a rapid decline, can lead to feelings of fatigue, decreased focus and diminished exercise performance. You might experience a sudden dip in energy, leaving you feeling tired and unfocused during your workout. Even worse, in a fasted state or after a crash, your body might resort to breaking down muscle tissue for fuel, hindering the very muscle growth and repair what you're striving for. Additionally, these crashes can trigger cravings for more readily available sugars, potentially leading to overeating and derailing your overall dietary goals.

Complex carbs, the champions of the carb's kingdom are what you should prioritize. Think whole grains like brown rice, quinoa and oats. Fruits like berries and apples and starchy vegetables like sweet potatoes and corn, all fall under this category. These complex carbs provide sustained energy, essential nutrients and fibre for optimal health and performance. Complex carbs act like a steady stream flowing into the river. They are digested more slowly, releasing glucose gradually into your bloodstream. This helps maintain balanced blood sugar levels, providing you with sustained energy throughout the day and during your workouts. By prioritizing complex carbs over simple ones, you can avoid the blood sugar roller coaster and ensure your body has the consistent fuel it needs to power your fitness journey. When it comes to carb selection, prioritize complex carbs over simple carbs. Focus on whole grains, fruits and starchy vegetables. These provide sustained energy, essential nutrients and fibre for optimal health and performance.

What are the benefits of Carbs?

Sharpening your mind: Carbs are the brain's preferred fuel source. Adequate carbohydrate intake ensures optimal cognitive function, focus and energy levels throughout the day. Carbohydrates play a critical role in supporting optimal cognitive function. The human brain, unlike other organs, relies heavily on glucose, a simple sugar derived from carbohydrates, as its primary fuel source. Studies have established a strong link between adequate carbohydrate intake and improved cognitive function in various areas. These include enhanced memory, focus, concentration and overall mental clarity. For individuals engaged in mentally demanding activities, such as students preparing for exams or professionals working long hours, ensuring sufficient carbohydrate intake can be a crucial factor in maintaining peak cognitive performance.

Fuelling Workouts: Complex carbs provide the long-lasting energy needed to push harder and longer during weight training and cardio sessions. For individuals focusing on weight training, complex carbohydrates are essential for replenishing muscle glycogen stores. Glycogen is the primary energy source for muscle contractions, and depletion during exercise can lead to fatigue and decreased performance.

Replenishing Muscle Glycogen: Your body utilizes muscle glycogen (stored carbohydrates) for energy during workouts. Replenishing these stores post-workout with complex carbs is crucial for muscle recovery and growth. During exercise, particularly high-intensity workouts, your body utilizes muscle glycogen for energy. As these stores become depleted, fatigue sets in, impacting your performance and hindering your ability to push your limits. Replenishing muscle glycogen stores post-workout is crucial for optimal recovery and future growth. Consuming complex carbohydrates post-workout provides the necessary fuel for muscle glycogen resynthesis, promoting optimal muscle recovery and growth. Complex carbohydrates, with their gradual release of glucose, provide a sustained source of energy for muscle glycogen resynthesis, allowing your muscles to rebuild and repair themselves more efficiently. This translates to faster recovery times, reduced muscle soreness, and the ability to return to your training regimen feeling stronger and more prepared for the next challenge.

Fats: The essential players

Fats have long been unfairly demonised, but they are essential macronutrients that play a vital role in overall health. Overall fats provide a concentrated source of energy, support hormone production and aid in the absorption of essential vitamins. There are three main types of fats, saturated, monounsaturated and polyunsaturated fats.

Saturated Fats: Found primarily in animal products like red meat, full-fat dairy and some plant-based sources like coconut oil. While not inherently bad, saturated fats should be consumed in moderation, favouring healthier fat sources will help you strike the right balance in your diet.

Monounsaturated Fats: Considered "healthy fats," monounsaturated fats are found in sources like avocados, olive oil, coconut oil, nuts and seeds. They can help lower bad cholesterol (LDL) and improve heart health keeping you performing at your best.

Polyunsaturated Fats: Another category of "healthy fats," polyunsaturated fats include omega-3 and omega-6 fatty acids. Omega-3s are particularly beneficial for reducing inflammation and promoting overall health. Fatty fish like salmon and tuna, flaxseeds and walnuts are all excellent sources of omega-3s.

Prioritize healthy fats like monounsaturated and polyunsaturated fats over saturated fats. Focus on incorporating sources like:

Avocados, the trendy superfood that has taken the culinary world by storm, are a fantastic source of healthy fats. These creamy delights are packed with monounsaturated fats, making them a delicious way to boost your intake.

Olive oil, a cornerstone of the heart-healthy Mediterranean diet, deserves a prominent place in your kitchen. This versatile oil is rich in monounsaturated fats and boasts anti-inflammatory properties. Drizzle it on salads or use it for cooking.

Nuts like almonds, walnuts and cashews are a fantastic source of healthy fats, protein, and fibre. They offer a convenient on-the-go snack or can be incorporated into meals for added texture and flavour. Just be mindful of portion sizes, as nuts are calorie dense.

Seeds. Flaxseeds and chia seeds are tiny nutritional powerhouses bursting with omega-3 fatty acids, a type of polyunsaturated fat crucial for reducing inflammation and promoting overall health. Sprinkle them on oatmeal, yoghurt, or even bake them into healthy treats.

Fatty fish such as salmon, tuna and sardines are delicious options rich in omega 3, promoting heart health and reducing inflammation.

What are the benefits of Fats?

Slow and steady energy: Unlike carbohydrates, fats are digested at a slower rate, providing a steady and long-lasting energy stream of energy. This is particularly beneficial for athletes who engage in endurance training like long cardio sessions. While carbohydrates are the preferred fuel source for high-intensity exercise, fats play a critical role in supporting sustained energy levels, particularly during endurance activities like long-distance cycling or running. Unlike carbohydrates, which are broken down and released as glucose relatively quickly, fats are digested at a slower rate. This translates to a gradual and prolonged release of energy into the bloodstream, providing a steady fuel source for extended periods of exercise.

Hormonal balance and muscle growth: Fats are essential to produce various hormones crucial for getting lean and toned, including testosterone. Testosterone plays a key role in muscle growth and development, impacting factors like protein synthesis and muscle repair, so ensuring adequate healthy fats in your diet supports this vital process.

Enhancing nutrient absorption of vitamins: Certain vitamins, like vitamins A, D, E, and K, are fat-soluble. This means they need fat for proper absorption into your body. By consuming adequate healthy fats, you ensure these essential vitamins, which play a role in everything from immune function to cell health, are properly absorbed and utilised. Consuming adequate amounts of healthy fats alongside these vitamins ensures they are effectively absorbed in the digestive tract and transported throughout the body. These fat-soluble vitamins play a vital role in various bodily functions, including immune health, cell health, and bone health. Optimizing their absorption through adequate healthy fat intake can contribute to overall well-being and support peak performance.

Cellular integrity and function: Fats are vital components of cell membranes, which act as the control centres of your cells, regulating what enters and leaves so in other words the flow of nutrients and waste products. Consuming healthy fats helps maintain the structure and function of these membranes, ensuring proper communication and signalling within your body. This efficient communication is essential for optimal bodily function, which translates for optimal bodily function, impacting everything from muscle contractions during exercise to the regulation of metabolic processes.

Improved satiety and appetite management: Like protein, healthy fats promote feelings of fullness and satiety. This means you will feel satisfied for longer after meals, potentially helping you manage your calorie intake more effectively. This can be particularly beneficial during periods of calorie restriction, for individuals engaged in bodybuilding or those following calorie-restricted diets. By feeling fuller for longer, you're less likely to experience cravings and overeat, making it easier to adhere to your dietary goals.

Chapter 3: Micronutrients, the powerhouse players

While macronutrients (carbs, proteins and fats) provide the bulk of your energy, micronutrients – including vitamins and minerals – play a crucial role in various bodily functions. They are essential for overall health, optimising training performance and maximizing your results.
Micronutrients do not directly fuel your workouts however they act as the invisible conductors, ensuring the smooth operation of vital processes.

What are the main functions of micronutrients?

Enzyme production: Micronutrients serve as cofactors for enzymes, which are biological catalysts that accelerate countless chemical reactions within your body. These reactions are essential for energy metabolism, hormone regulation and muscle function. Deficiencies in certain micronutrients can hinder enzyme production, potentially leading to fatigue and compromised performance.

Hormone regulation: Maintaining a healthy hormonal balance is crucial. Micronutrients play a vital role in the production and regulation of hormones like testosterone, which is essential for muscle growth and development. Additionally, vitamins and minerals contribute to the production of hormones that regulate metabolism, sleep quality, and recovery.

Immune system function: A robust immune system is vital to fight off infections and recover effectively from intense training sessions. Micronutrients like vitamin C, zinc and iron play a crucial role in immune system function, helping you stay healthy and focused on your goals.

Nutrient absorption: Some vitamins, like vitamin A, are fat-soluble. This means they require fats for proper absorption from the digestive tract. Consuming adequate dietary fats ensures you maximize the benefits of these essential vitamins.

Overall health and well-being: Micronutrients contribute to various bodily functions, including bone health, nervous system function, and maintaining healthy blood pressure. Deficiencies in certain micronutrients can lead to fatigue, decreased immunity and hinder your overall health. Now that you understand the importance of micronutrients, let's delve deeper into the specific vitamins and minerals:

Vitamins

Vitamin A: Crucial for vision, vitamin A also plays a role in immune function and cell differentiation, which is essential for muscle growth and repair. Rich sources include sweet potatoes, carrots and leafy green vegetables such as kale, spinach, collard greens and Swiss chard.

B Vitamins (B1, B2, B3, B6, B12): This group of vitamins plays a vital role in energy metabolism, converting food into usable energy for your workouts. Additionally, B vitamins contribute to nervous system function and maintaining healthy red blood cells for optimal oxygen transport. Excellent sources include whole grains, legumes, lean meats and eggs.

Vitamin C: A powerful antioxidant, vitamin C supports immune system function and helps reduce inflammation caused by exercise. It also contributes to collagen synthesis, which is a key component of connective tissues. Citrus fruits, leafy greens and sweet peppers are rich sources of vitamin C.

Vitamin D: Often referred to as the "sunshine vitamin," vitamin D plays a crucial role in bone health and calcium absorption. It also contributes to muscle function and immune system function. Fatty fish and eggs are good sources of vitamin D.

Minerals

Calcium: The primary mineral for building strong bones and teeth, calcium also plays a role in muscle function and nerve transmission. Dairy products, leafy green vegetables, and fortified foods like tofu are rich sources of calcium.

Magnesium: Essential for muscle function and recovery, magnesium contributes to protein synthesis and helps regulate blood sugar levels. Nuts, seeds, legumes, and dark leafy greens are excellent sources of magnesium.

Iron: A vital component of red blood cells, iron is crucial for transporting oxygen throughout the body, ensuring optimal delivery to your muscles during workouts. Lean meats, poultry, fish, beans, and lentils are rich sources of iron.

Zinc: This mineral plays a role in protein synthesis, wound healing, and immune function. It also contributes to testosterone production. Oysters, red meat, poultry and pumpkin seeds are good sources of zinc.

Chapter 4: Tips from Champions & trouble shooting

This chapter delves into the strategies and routines employed by the elite, equipping you with the knowledge and tools to elevate your own fitness journey which is not without its hurdles. Here's how champions navigate common challenges.

Champion Routines and Mindset for unwavering motivation

Cultivate a champion mindset: Fitness is not just about physical transformation, first it's about cultivating a champion mindset. This means fostering unwavering belief in yourself, embracing challenges with a positive attitude and staying focused on long-term progress. Champion mindset is about progress, not perfection. Celebrate small wins and setbacks are inevitable but they are also opportunities to learn and grow. Building a sculpted physique requires dedication and a clear roadmap to success. That's where S.M.A.R.T. goal setting comes in.

Set S.M.A.R.T. goals: specific, measurable, achievable, relevant and time-bound goals provide direction and a sense of accomplishment.

S - Specific: Aim high but aim precisely
You regularly need to set realistic goals and when you set them, don't just say "get stronger" or "lose weight." Be more specific! For example, "Increase my bench press by 5kg (around 11lbs) in the next 3 months" or "reduce my body fat percentage by 2% within 6 months" these are clear and specific goals you can work towards. I strongly suggest you buy a body composition scale, it is a great help to monitor your progress over time. It measures your weight, body fat percentage and muscle mass and you can easily find it in large online retailers or in specialist fitness sports stores.

M - Measurable: Track your progress and celebrate wins
How will you know if you're reaching your goals? It is very important to integrate measurable elements. Celebrating victories, big or small, keeps your momentum going. Acknowledge and reward yourself for reaching those milestones.
<u>Track your weight once a week</u> and not every day. Building muscle and reducing fat is a beautiful dance, not a straight line down. You might be shedding fat while simultaneously building muscle, which can mask progress on the scale. Daily weigh-ins can be discouraging, overlooking this crucial body re-composition. In addition, factors like hydration, sodium intake and even your workout schedule can cause daily weight fluctuations.
Take progress pictures at set intervals. Sometimes, the scale and the mirror don't tell the whole story. Progress pictures, however, paint a clear representation. By capturing yourself at set intervals (every 2-3 weeks is ideal), you can visually see the changes in your body composition.
<u>Take progress pictures</u> at regular intervals, perhaps once a month or every six weeks. While the scale can be a discouraging metric at times, progress pictures don't lie. Witnessing the physical changes that you are making over time can be a huge motivator and a reminder of how far you've come. For consistency, try to take pictures in the same lighting conditions and using the same pose

each time. This allows for a more accurate visual comparison. Most importantly, own your progress! Be proud of the effort you are putting in and the results you are achieving.

Get your physical measurements. Ideally take measurements in the morning, this helps to minimize water weight fluctuations that can occur throughout the day. I suggest using a fabric tape measure which is more flexible than metal ones. I invite you to download the bonus schedule I prepared for you, just scroll to the bonus page at the end of the book.

Chest: Measure around the fullest part of your chest, usually just above the nipples. Keep the tape measure level and parallel to the ground. Relax your arms by your sides and breathe normally. Shoulders: There are two ways to measure shoulders, around or cross: around measuring around the widest part of your shoulders, including your upper arms. This provides a general idea of your upper body size. Otherwise, cross standing with your arms relaxed at your sides. Measure from the outermost point of one shoulder to the outermost point of the other.

Waist: Measure around your natural waistline, typically above your hip bones but below your ribs. Don't hold your breath or suck in your stomach – aim for a relaxed measurement.

Hips: Measure around the widest part of your hips, including your glutes. Keep your feet hip-width apart and stand tall.

Biceps (flexed): Find the peak of your bicep when your arm is flexed at a 90-degree angle. Measure around the fullest part of your flexed bicep.

Thighs (flexed): Like biceps, find the fullest part of your quadriceps when your leg is slightly bent at the knee. Measure around the thickest part of your flexed thigh.

Calves: Stand with your weight on one leg and the other slightly bent behind you. Measure around the thickest part of your calf muscle.

Seeing these tangible improvements is a fantastic motivator and reminds you of how far you've come.

Track your workout journal where you can record details like exercises performed, sets, reps, weights used and even how you felt during the session.

If you scroll down to the end of the book you will find the workout journal for you to download and update. Over time, this journal transforms into a testament to your dedication and serves as a valuable resource to track your progress and plan future workouts. Scroll down to the end of the book to find the bonus body measurement tracker.

A - Achievable: Challenge yourself but be realistic
Setting short term goals that are too ambitious can lead to discouragement. Be honest with yourself about your current fitness level and set achievable targets. Think of it like climbing a mountain – you wouldn't attempt Everest straight away, plan you're a
scent with achievable milestones along the way. Assess your current fitness level realistically. Are you a complete beginner or do you have some experience? For example, instead of aiming to squat 100kg (220lbs) if you can currently only manage 50kg (110lbs), set a goal to increase your squat by 5kg (11lbs) every 4 weeks.

R - Relevant: Goals aligned with your big picture

Before setting specific goals, take a step back and define your ultimate long-term aspirations. Do you dream of competing on stage? Are you aiming to lose some weight and obtain a toned and defined body?
Are your goals in line with your overall vision? For example, if your ultimate goal is to compete in a bodybuilding competition, your training goals might be more specific to building muscle mass and definition.

T - Time-Bound: Set deadlines for milestones

Every goal needs a deadline. This creates a sense of urgency and keeps you focused. For example, instead of simply saying "get leaner," aim to "reduce my body fat percentage by 2% within 6 months." Having a timeframe motivates you to stay on track and celebrate achieving milestones. Consider your experience, beginners might need longer deadlines compared to seasoned gym-goers. Be realistic about the time it takes to achieve your goals.

Short term goals (1-4 weeks) are especially important to develop a safe and effective fitness program with a qualified personal trainer. This will ensure you learn all the movements well, focusing on proper depth, back position and knee alignment for exercises like squats within 2 weeks. This way, you'll build a strong foundation for future progress and minimize the risk of injury. If you're a beginner, aim to do 1 to 2 extra reps of bodyweight exercises like lunges or push-ups within 4 weeks. By prioritizing quality movement over quantity in the short term, you'll establish a solid foundation for long-term success.

Mid-term goals (4-8 weeks) are ideal for reducing body fat percentage, building muscle mass or improving overall fitness. You might aim to increase weight training intensity and introduce new exercises.

Long term goals (8+ weeks) are perfect for major transformations or competition prep.

Find a training partner: Having a supportive partner keeps you accountable and adds a social element to your workouts. We all have those days where the sofa beckons more than the barbell. A training partner acts as your accountability anchor. Knowing someone is relying on you to show up keeps you motivated and ensures you don't skip workouts on a whim. With a training partner, your workouts can become a social event. You can chat, share training tips, motivate each other and maybe even have a laugh or two (between sets, of course!). This social element can make a huge difference in keeping you engaged and enjoying the gym experience. Also, Training with a partner who shares your goals can elevate your workouts to a whole new level. You can spot each other, push each other to lift heavier weights, and offer constructive criticism to improve form. The ideal training partner isn't just someone who lifts the same weight as you. Look for someone who shares your goals, motivates you and most importantly, someone you enjoy spending time with.

Visualize Success: Take time each day to visualize yourself achieving your goals. Vivid imagery can be a powerful motivator. Elite athletes across various disciplines swear by the power of visualization. It's about taking a mental snapshot of yourself achieving your goals. This could involve picturing yourself hitting a new personal best lift, achieving impressive muscle definition or simply feeling strong and confident on stage. Don't just see it – feel it! Visualize yourself performing lifts, feeling the weight in your hands, the pump in your muscles and the satisfying burn as you push your limits. Visualization is not just about daydreaming. Studies suggest it can prime your nervous system and improve muscular coordination. Just like your workouts, aim for regular visualization sessions. Dedicate 5 minutes each day to picturing yourself achieving your goals.

Seek Inspiration: Surround yourself with positive influences. Follow inspiring athletes online, read bodybuilding or fitness related magazines or watch motivational videos.
Feeling uninspired? Dive into the world of fitness documentaries or inspirational fitness films. Witnessing the dedication, discipline, and incredible transformations of other athletes can reignite your own passion and remind you of what's possible with hard work. Whether it's bodybuilding magazines, documentaries, or local success stories, actively seek out sources of inspiration that keep you fired up and focused on achieving your goals.

Focus on progress, not perfection: Don't get discouraged by setbacks. Celebrate small wins and focus on consistent progress, not achieving perfection overnight. Social media and glossy magazines can paint an unrealistic picture of bodybuilding – flawless physiques sculpted overnight. But remember, these are often the endpoint of years of dedicated training, not a starting point. Don't get discouraged by unrealistic expectations. Focus on making consistent progress, no matter how small and celebrate those wins – that's the key to long-term success. Every extra rep on a lift, every kilo shed, every improvement in form – these are all victories! Acknowledge these milestones, no matter how seemingly insignificant. Treat yourself to a healthy reward, write it down in your workout journal or simply give yourself a mental pat on the back.

Pre and post workout nutrition

Nutrition plays a crucial role in optimizing your workouts and recovery. Here's a general guideline:

Pre-Workout Meal: Consume a meal rich in complex carbohydrates and moderate protein 1-2 hours before training to provide sustained energy. The ideal pre-workout meal is a strategic alliance between complex carbohydrates and moderate protein, consumed 1-2 hours before your workout training in the gym. An example is a banana with a tablespoon of peanut butter. This classic combo provides quick energy (carbs from banana) and muscle-building protein from peanut butter.

Post-Workout Meal: Within 30 minutes after your workout, consume a combination of protein and carbohydrates to kickstart muscle repair and replenish glycogen stores. These protein warriors get to work immediately, patching up those tiny tears, laying the foundation for stronger, more resilient muscle growth. But protein is not enough. Enter complex carbohydrates as well as these slow-digesting carbs provide a steady stream of energy, refilling your glycogen reserves and ensuring your body has the resources it needs to recover effectively. An example is a protein shake with fruit. A quick and convenient option. Choose a protein powder without added sugar and blend it with water or milk and your favourite fruit.

Rest and Recovery

Just as important as intense training is dedicated rest and recovery. During rest periods, your body repairs muscle tissue, replenishes energy stores and adapts to the training stimulus, leading to stronger, bigger muscles. Here's how champions prioritize recovery:

Better sleep, better results: Aim for 7-8 hours of quality sleep each night. Sleep deprivation hinders muscle growth and recovery. When you drift off to sleep, your body enters a state of repair. During this precious time, muscle tissues that were challenged during your workout begin to rebuild and strengthen. Sleep deprivation disrupts this vital repair process, hindering muscle growth and recovery. In addition, the growth hormone, a key player in muscle growth and development, is released in significant quantities during deep sleep. Skimping on sleep means a dip in growth hormone production, putting a damper on your progress. Also, intense training can put a strain on your body, leading to increased stress levels. Sleep acts as a natural stress reliever, allowing your body and mind to de-stress and recharge. This translates to better recovery, improved mood, and a more resilient training experience.

Active Recovery: This isn't about sitting on the couch and watching telly! It's about incorporating gentle activities between your intense training sessions to promote blood flow and aid muscle recovery. Light activity like walking or stretching deliver essential nutrients and oxygen to aid repair, speeding up the recovery process and reducing muscle soreness – so you can get back to the gym feeling fresher and stronger. Active recovery routines incorporating light stretches or mobility exercises help maintain flexibility and prevent injuries. Some excellent options for active recovery that you can easily incorporate into your routine other than stretching can be walking, light cardio like a gentle swim, cycling session or other low impact activities such as Pilates to improve flexibility and core strength. However, don't overdo it! Active recovery should feel good, not like another intense workout, choose activities that promote relaxation and gentle movement.

Listen to Your Body: Don't push through excessive pain or fatigue. Building an impressive physique requires dedication and pushing your limits, but there's a fine line between dedication and disaster. While some muscle soreness is normal after a tough workout, excessive pain is a warning sign. Pushing through severe pain can lead to injuries that sideline you for weeks, hindering your progress. Remember, your body is talking – listen to it! Take a step back, rest and allow your body to recover properly. Schedule rest days and reload weeks (reduced training intensity) to prevent overtraining and injuries and to allow muscles to repair and rebuild. Just like your phone needs charging, your body needs rest days. Think of it as giving your body time to catch its breath and come back stronger for the next training session.

Clean eating, cheating and dealing with cravings

Clean eating.
Focus on whole food limiting processed food and learn to read labels: Clean eating prioritizes whole, unprocessed foods over refined options. This is about a return departure from the processed, packaged world. Instead of sugary drinks, quench your thirst with water infused with fresh lemons or berries. Swap greasy takeout for salmon fillets bursting with omega-3 fatty acids. Ditch the white bread and pastries in favour of whole-wheat options that keep you feeling fuller for longer. Fruits, vegetables, lean proteins, whole grains and healthy fats form the basis of a clean eating plan. Processed foods are often high in sugar, unhealthy fats and sodium, hindering your goals. Become familiar with food labels to make informed choices and avoid hidden sugars and unhealthy ingredients. Food labels become your blueprints, revealing the hidden ingredients lurking within packaged foods. Learn to decipher the numbers, understand the difference between healthy fats and their unhealthy counterparts, and become familiar with sneaky sugars hiding under unfamiliar names. With this knowledge, you can make informed choices, avoiding hidden nasties that can derail your progress.

Start eating vegetables first: The veggies-first approach helps manage blood sugar levels. When you introduce vegetables first, your body starts processing them right away. Sugary or processed foods often cause blood sugar spikes followed by crashes. This energy rollercoaster can leave you feeling sluggish and hinder your gym performance. Veggies, on the other hand, are generally low in sugar and help regulate blood sugar for sustained energy throughout the day. When you consume sugary or processed foods first, your body releases a surge of insulin, a hormone that helps shuttle sugar from your bloodstream into your cells. This rapid rise in blood sugar is followed by a crash as your body overcompensates and produces too much insulin. Secondly, vegetables are packed with fibre that slow down the absorption of sugar from other foods you eat later in the meal.

Cheating, how often is "often enough"? There is no one-size-fits all answer to cheat meal frequency. It depends on your individual goals, metabolism and activity level. A good rule of thumb is to limit cheat meals to once or twice every week, ideally in the weekend. Since you've got your meals prepped for lunch and dinner during the week, weekends naturally offer more flexibility. Saturday and Sundays are often filled with social gatherings and family meals. A couple of cheat meals on Saturday and/or Sunday allow you to enjoy these occasions without feeling restricted or missing out. Sticking to a strict meal plan all week can be mentally draining. A weekend cheat meal provides a well-deserved break from counting macros and portion control, allowing you to come back to your healthy eating plan feeling refreshed and motivated. I advise to choose a specific meal you truly crave, rather than mindless overeating. The key to a successful cheat meal is getting back on track quickly. Even with cheat meals, practice mindful eating. Savour the flavours and stop when you are comfortably satisfied, not stuffed. The next meal: aim for a clean and balanced high-protein meal following your cheat. This does not have to be a drastic calorie reduction but prioritize lean protein, healthy fats and complex carbohydrates to replenish your body with the nutrients it needs. Treat the cheat meal as a single indulgence and continue with your regular healthy eating plan the next day. Cheat meals can be a valuable tool in your fitness journey. They can provide a mental break from strict dieting, boost your metabolism and even help you stay on track long-term. Used strategically, they can be delicious and motivating.

Find healthy alternatives: Satisfy cravings with healthier options like fruits, low-fat yogurt with berries or dark chocolate. Planning is key, having healthy snacks readily available helps you avoid grabbing unhealthy options when cravings strike. Prepare chopped fruits and vegetables in advance or keep individual portions of yoghurt and nuts handy. Reach for a juicy apple, a handful of berries, some sliced mango, or a refreshing grapefruit when a sugar craving hits. These fruits are naturally sweet and packed with vitamins, minerals and fibre, keeping you feeling satisfied.

Sometimes, a savoury craving can masquerade as a sweet one. If you're yearning for something with a bit of a kick, try a handful of roasted chickpeas seasoned with paprika and cayenne pepper, or some sliced cucumber with a sprinkle of chilli flakes and lime juice. These healthy snacks are bursting with flavour and can help curb cravings in a surprising way.

Craving chocolate? Indulge in a square or two of dark chocolate (70% cocoa content or higher) instead of reaching for a sugary milk chocolate bar. Dark chocolate is rich in antioxidants and can help satisfy your sweet tooth without sabotaging your progress.

Hydration is key: Dehydration can sometimes mimic cravings. Ensure you are properly hydrated throughout the day. Water is essential for pretty much everything your body does, including regulating your metabolism and keeping you feeling energised. When you are dehydrated, your body might send signals that feel like hunger pangs or cravings. Reaching for a glass of water instead of a sugary snack could be all it takes to silence those urges. Dehydration can often manifest as headaches, fatigue, and yes, even cravings. If you are feeling a sudden urge to snack, especially for sugary treats, try downing a glass of water first. Make staying hydrated a convenient habit. Keep a reusable water bottle with you throughout the day and aim to finish it multiple times. This way, you will always have water on hand to quench your thirst and avoid reaching for sugary drinks or unhealthy snacks. Sip on water throughout your training session to stay hydrated and prevent muscle fatigue. Again, remember carrying a reusable water bottle to the gym makes this easy and ensures you are replenishing fluids as you sweat.

Mindful Eating: Eat slowly and savour your food, paying attention to hunger cues to avoid overeating. Mindful eating is about slowing down and savouring the experience. Put down your phone, turn off the TV and focus on your meal. This allows you to appreciate the taste, texture, and aroma of your food, making the experience more enjoyable and helping you recognise fullness cues earlier. We often underestimate the power of proper chewing. When you rush through your meals, you don't give your body enough time to register satiety signals.

Mindful eating is also about reconnecting with your body's natural hunger and fullness cues. Before reaching for seconds, ask yourself – am I truly hungry, or am I just bored, stressed, or eating out of habit? Listen to the body's hunger cues and stop eating when you are comfortably full, not stuffed.

Meditation for body and mind

Meditation offers numerous benefits including:

Stress reduction: Chronic stress can hinder progress. Meditation helps manage stress, promoting better sleep and recovery. Building a sculpted physique requires dedication in the gym but what happens outside the gym walls can significantly impact your progress. Chronic stress can wreak havoc on your sleep, recovery and ultimately your goals. That is where incorporating stress management techniques, like meditation, becomes your secret weapon. Chronic stress elevates cortisol levels, a hormone that can lead to muscle breakdown and hinder your ability to build muscle. It can also disrupt sleep patterns, crucial for muscle repair and recovery. By managing stress, you are creating an environment that optimises your body for success. Meditation is an ancient practice that has gained widespread popularity in recent times and for good reason. Regular meditation sessions can significantly reduce stress and anxiety. As you focus on your breath and quiet your mind, your body enters a state of deep relaxation, promoting feelings of calmness and well-being. There's no one-size-fits-all approach to meditation. Explore different techniques to find what works best for you. Guided meditations are a great starting point, with calming voices or soft music leading you through relaxation exercises. Experiment and find a technique that brings you a sense of inner peace. Simple breathing exercises can be incorporated throughout your day to manage stress in the moment. Try mindful breathing, take slow, deep breaths through your nose, filling your belly with air and hold for a count of three before exhaling slowly through your mouth. Repeat this for a few minutes whenever you feel stress creeping in.

Mind-muscle connection: Mindfulness exercises can improve the mind-muscle connection, allowing you to better control and target specific muscle groups during training. Building a lean and toned body is about more than just lifting weights; it's about connecting your mind with your muscles. Meditation cultivates a heightened sense of awareness, allowing you to feel your muscles working with each movement. This mind-muscle connection is crucial for proper form execution and maximizing muscle growth. Think of meditation as a bridge between your mind and body, ensuring every rep targets the intended muscles for optimal results. Meditation helps you cultivate a state of mindfulness, a state of being fully present in the moment. This translates to the gym as a sense of flow, where you're completely absorbed in your workout. Each rep becomes deliberate and controlled, and you're less likely to rush through your sets just to get it over with. This mindful approach allows you to truly connect with your body and experience the joy of movement. Overall, by incorporating meditation into your routine, you're not just calming your mind, you are sharpening your focus and concentration, which translates to more productive and rewarding gym sessions.

Chapter 5: Individual macro split and portion control

Unlike a one-size-fits-all approach, portion control requires personalisation. Your ideal portion sizes will depend on several factors, including:

Bodyweight and body composition: Larger individuals naturally have higher calorie requirements than individuals with smaller builds. Your body composition, consisting of muscle mass and fat mass, also plays a role. Muscle tissue burns more calories at rest than fat tissue, so someone with a higher muscle mass may require more calories overall.

Individual goals: Are you aiming for muscle building (calorie surplus), fat loss (calorie deficit), or maintaining your current physique (calorie maintenance)? Your goals significantly impact your portion control strategy. A calorie surplus is needed for muscle gain, while a calorie deficit is necessary for fat loss.

Activity level: The intensity and duration of your training sessions influence your calorie needs. Highly active bodybuilders will require more calories to fuel their workouts and support recovery compared to those with less intense training schedules

But how do you determine the perfect amount of fuel for your unique engine? This is where three crucial concepts come into play: Basal Metabolic Rate (BMR), Total Daily Energy Expenditure (TDEE), and Lean Body Mass (LBM). Understanding these concepts unlocks the secrets to portion control and empowers you to take charge of your fitness journey.

Bmr: The Engine's Idle – What it is and why it matters

BMR is the number of calories your body burns at rest, simply to maintain its basic functions. It encompasses the essential functions that keep you alive and breathing, even when you're binging on the couch!

Your BMR is influenced by several factors:

- **Body Composition:** Muscle tissue burns more calories at rest compared to fat tissue. So, someone with a higher muscle mass naturally has a higher BMR.
- **Age:** Generally, BMR tends to decrease with age due to a decline in muscle mass and metabolic rate.
- **Sex:** Men typically have a higher BMR than women due to larger muscle mass.
- **Genetics:** Some lucky individuals are genetically predisposed to a higher BMR, while others may have a naturally lower one.

Knowing your BMR is a crucial first step in calculating your ideal calorie intake. It provides a baseline for understanding how many calories your body burns simply by existing. Here's the catch: your BMR doesn't tell the whole story. While there's a single concept of Basal Metabolic Rate, there are actually a few different formulas used to estimate it. The two most popular ones are:

- The Mifflin St Jeor Equation: This is the current gold standard for BMR calculations, considering factors like age, weight, height and sex.
- The Revised Harris-Benedict Equation: This is an older formula, but still widely used. It uses similar factors as the Mifflin St Jeor equation but may yield slightly different results.

Using the Mifflin St Jeor equation here is the formula to use. Weight should be entered in kilograms (kg) and height in centimetres (cm):

BMR (men) = 10 * weight (kg) + 6.25 * height (cm) - 5 * age (years) + 5
BMR (women) = 10 * weight (kg) + 6.25 * height (cm) - 5 * age (years) - 161
You can easily calculate your BMR, there are several free online calculators that can help you estimate your BMR based on your age, sex, height, and weight.

Tdee: The Real-world fuel gauge, unveiling your daily needs

Your BMR only considers your body's calorie burn at rest. You need to factor in your daily activity level to estimate your Total Daily Energy Expenditure (TDEE). is your body's engine idling in the garage, your TDEE reflects real-world fuel consumption. TDEE is the total number of calories your body burns in a day, which takes your BMR and adds the calories burned through activity. These activities include:

- **Exercise:** Your workouts significantly impact your TDEE. The intensity and duration of your training sessions determine how many extra calories you burn.
- **Non-Exercise Activity Thermogenesis (NEAT):** This refers to the calories you burn through everyday activities like walking, fidgeting, and even cleaning the house.
- **The Thermic Effect of Food (TEF):** The body burns a small portion of calories simply digesting and absorbing nutrients from your food.

Here's the equation for calculating your TDEE:

TDEE = BMR x Activity Level Factor
In other words, multiply your BMR by the activity level factor corresponding to your lifestyle. This will give you your estimated TDEE, which is the total number of calories your body burns in a day.

Activity Level Factors:

- Sedentary (little to no exercise): BMR x 1.2
- Lightly active (light exercise/sports 1-3 days/week): BMR x 1.375
- Moderately active (moderate exercise/sports 3-5 days/week): BMR x 1.55
- Very active (hard exercise/sports 6-7 days/week): BMR x 1.725
- Extremely active (very hard exercise/sports & physical job): BMR x 1.9

This explanation of BMR and TDEE equips you with the foundational knowledge to understand your body's unique calorie needs. To simplify and personalize your portion control journey, head over to my website at www.fitnessmealprep.com and head to the macros calculator. There, you'll find the macros calculator designed to calculate your daily calorie and macronutrient needs a breeze. As a matter of fact, it considers your individual BMR, activity level and your goals to provide a personalized roadmap for fuelling your progress. Whether you're aiming for muscle building, fat loss or maintenance, the macros calculator offers a convenient and efficient way to tailor your nutrition for optimal results.

How do you choose the right macros split?

The best macro split for you depends on several factors including your individual goals, activity level, health status, BMR and TDEE. Are you trying to lose weight, gain muscle or maintain your weight? Your goals will influence how you split your macros within your TDEE.
Weight loss: you'll need to create a calorie deficit by consuming fewer calories than your TDEE. How much of a deficit depends on your goals and health status. Your macro split can help you achieve that deficit in a healthy way. You can subtract 250-500 calories from your TDEE for a gradual weight loss.
Muscle gain: you'll need a calorie surplus by consuming more calories than your TDEE. Again, your macro split can help you achieve that surplus while providing the building blocks for muscle growth (protein). You can add 250-500 calories to your TDEE for a gradual muscle gain.
Maintenance: here, you'll aim to consume roughly the same number of calories as your TDEE.
Here is a more detailed breakdown of which split might be suitable for various fitness goals:

<u>**Cutting (Losing Weight):**</u>

Focus: Create a calorie deficit (burning more calories than you consume) to promote fat loss while preserving muscle mass. The following macro split allows you to create a calorie deficit for weight loss while still feeling satisfied and getting the nutrients your body needs.
Individual Needs: Adjust protein intake slightly higher based on your activity level and goals.
Nutrient Adequacy: Ensure you're getting enough fruits, vegetables and whole grains for essential vitamins and minerals.
Sustainability: Focus on whole, unprocessed foods to create a diet you can stick to long-term.

Macro split:

- **Balanced high protein (40% Carbs / 30% Protein / 30% Fat):** This provides a good foundation for nutrient intake while allowing for calorie restriction. You can adjust portion sizes within this split to achieve a deficit.
- **Moderate Protein (40% Carbs / 40% Protein / 20% Fat):** This split prioritizes protein to help maintain muscle mass during a calorie deficit.

Bulking (Gaining Muscle):

Focus: Create a calorie surplus (consuming more calories than you burn) to support muscle growth and repair.
Track Your Calories: Monitor your intake and adjust portions to achieve a slight surplus (250-500 calories per day).
Protein Needs: Aim for 0.8-1 gram of protein per pound of bodyweight to support muscle growth.

Macro split:

- **Balanced high protein (40% Carbs / 30% Protein / 30% Fat):** This can be a starting point, but you might need to adjust based on your activity level and goals.
- **Moderate Protein (40% Carbs / 40% Protein / 20% Fat):** This increases protein intake for muscle growth.
- **Higher Protein (30% Carbs / 50% Protein / 20% Fat):** This is an advanced approach for experienced bodybuilders, ideally consult a healthcare professional before adopting.

Maintenance (Maintaining body mass weight):

Focus: Consume enough calories to maintain your current weight and body composition.
Track Your Calories: Like bulking, tracking your calorie intake for a short period can help you establish your maintenance level. Aim to consume roughly the same number of calories you burn each day. There can be slight fluctuations, but if you notice significant weight gain or loss, adjust your calorie intake accordingly.
Protein Needs: While in maintenance, your protein needs may be slightly lower than when bulking. A range of 0.8-1.2 grams of protein per kilogram of bodyweight (around 0.36-0.54 grams per pound) is generally recommended for maintaining muscle mass.

Macro split: This can vary depending on your activity level and goals, but here are some options:

- **Balanced high protein (40% Carbs / 30% Protein / 30% Fat):** A versatile and sustainable approach for many people.
- **Slightly Higher Carbs (50% Carbs / 30% Protein / 20% Fat):** Suitable for individuals with active lifestyles who require more energy from carbohydrates.

Let's recap the various macros split:

Balanced high protein (40% Carbs / 30% Protein / 30% Fat):

This is a versatile widely recommended macro split, especially for beginners. It provides a good balance of all three macronutrients (proteins, carbs and fats) for overall health, energy, muscle building and hormone regulation. A balanced diet that incorporates all essential food groups (protein, carbohydrates, healthy fats, fruits, vegetables) is generally more sustainable in the long run compared to restrictive fad diets. This balanced high-protein macro split provides a versatile foundation for cutting, bulking or maintaining weight, depending on your overall calorie intake.

Low Fat (40% Carbs / 40% Protein / 20% Fat):

This split can be suitable for individuals who are bulking muscle while trying to minimize fat gain. It prioritizes protein for muscle building and keeps fat intake lower. While some resources advocate for this split for bulking with minimal fat gain, it's important to note that healthy fats are crucial for hormone production and satiety. A slightly higher fat intake (around 25-30%) might be more sustainable and beneficial.

Very High Protein (25% Carbs / 40% Protein / 35% Fats):

This protein-rich approach is commonly used during cutting phases to preserve muscle mass while restricting calories. The high protein intake helps maintain muscle mass during a calorie deficit. However, this split might not be ideal for everyone, especially those new to exercise or with certain health conditions.

High Carb (55% Carbs / 25% Protein / 20% Fat):

This split prioritizes carbohydrates, the primary energy source for the body, particularly during intense training. It might be suitable for athletes or individuals engaged in high-volume endurance activities. However, this approach might not be ideal for building muscle or weight loss goals.

Keto (5% Carbs / 25% Protein / 70% Fat):

This is a very low-carb, high-fat diet that forces the body to use fat for energy (ketosis). While some people use it for weight loss, it's a restrictive approach and might not be sustainable or suitable for everyone; bodybuilders normally prioritize protein and complex carbohydrates for muscle growth and recovery, which the keto diet minimizes.

Here's a table summarizing the macros splits and their potential applications:

Macro Split	Focus	Suitable For	Considerations
Balanced high protein (40% Carbs / 30% Protein / 30% Fat)	All-around health, muscle building	Beginners and general fitness goals	Versatile and sustainable for most people
Low Fat (40% Carbs / 40% Protein / 20% Fat)	Building muscle with minimal fat gain	Bulking with a focus on lean muscle	May be challenging to maintain satiety
Very High Protein (20% Carbs / 50% Protein / 30% Fats)	Muscle preservation during calorie deficit	Cutting phases for bodybuilders	Possible kidney strains in the long run
High Carb (55% Carbs / 25% Protein / 20% Fat)	Fuelling intense training	Athletes, endurance activities	Might not be ideal for building muscle or weight loss
Keto (5% Carbs / 25% Protein / 70% Fat)	Weight loss	People who want to lose weight	Not recommended for everyone, especially athletes

How do you adapt a recipe to your selected macros split?

The recipes in this meal prep plan guide are designed to roughly adapt to a balanced high protein macro split (40%carbs, 30%protein, 30%fat). These recipes provide a good foundation for most people so you can enjoy them as-is without worrying about precise calculations. Individual meals might vary slightly in their macronutrient (carbs, protein, fat) content. However, the overall meal plan is designed to provide a good balance of these nutrients throughout the workweek. The balanced high protein macro split approach is versatile and works well for various fitness goals like cutting, bulking or maintaining weight. There are several apps to track the macronutrients you have during the day to monitor or to calculate your daily macronutrient intake of carbs, protein and fat. However, if you're following a different macro split with specific ratios (e.g. higher protein for bulking), you can easily adapt these recipes.

Please head to my website www.fitnessmealprep.com to the macros calculator and insert your data, height, weight, activity level, nutrition goal and macro split.

How do you adapt a recipe to your macro breakdown and daily allowance?

Now, let's take an example with the following details:

Macro breakdown
Carbs: 204 grams/day
Protein: 153 grams/day
Fat: 68 grams/day

Daily calorie allowance
Total: 2,041 kcal/day
From carbs: 816 kcal/day
From protein: 612 kcal/day
From fat: 612 kcal/day

STEP BY STEP INSTRUCTIONS

1. Identify recipe macros. Look for the recipe's total calories, carbs, protein and fat content.

2. Compare recipe macros to your unique daily needs and see how much each recipe contributes to their daily macro goals:

Carbs: Divide recipe carbs (grams) by your daily carb target (204g) and multiply by 100% to get a percentage.

Protein: Same as carbs - divide recipe protein (grams) by your daily protein target (153g) and multiply by 100%.

Fat: Same as carbs - divide recipe fat (grams) by your daily fat target (68g) and multiply by 100%.

3. Adjust Portion Size or Ingredients (Simple Approach):

Recipe fits well: If the recipe's contribution to each macro falls within a reasonable range (around 20-30% of your daily target), you can enjoy it as is.

Recipe is higher in a specific macro:

- Reduce portion size: If a recipe is high in a macro, you need less of (e.g., carbs), eat a smaller portion. This could indicate reducing the portion size by 20-30% if a recipe significantly exceeds your desired macro intake for that meal.
- Substitute ingredients: Swap high-macro ingredients for lower-macro-ones (e.g., cauliflower rice instead of regular rice for lower carbs).

Recipe is lower in a specific macro:

- Increase portion size: If a recipe is low in a macro, you need more of (e.g., protein), eat a larger portion. Conversely, increasing the portion size by 20-30% might be appropriate if the recipe falls well below your desired macro intake.
- Add ingredients: Include ingredients high in that macro (e.g., grilled chicken for protein).

Now let's take a recipe that has 50g carbs, 20g protein and 30g fat (see macro breakdown above).
Carbs: This recipe contributes 50g / 204g = 25% of your daily carbs. It might be a good portion size.
Protein: This recipe contributes 20g / 153g = 13% of your daily protein. You might consider a slightly larger portion or adding a protein source on the side.

Fat: This recipe contributes 30g / 68g = 44% of your daily fat. It falls within a reasonable range for this example.

Overall, my suggestion is not to get overly stressed about hitting exact numbers. The most important thing is to find a sustainable and enjoyable way to eat healthy. I recommend starting with the recipes in our meal prep plan as is. As you follow the plan and monitor your body's response, you can then adjust portion sizes or substitute ingredients to better align with your individual needs and goals. This approach allows you to listen to your body and fine-tune your macros over time.

DOES THIS MEAL PREP PLAN WORK FOR EVERYONE, BOTH MEN AND WOMEN?
Yes absolutely! The meal prep plan itself likely won't need drastic changes for women but the portion sizes and potentially the macro targets within those portions might need some adjustments. The recipes themselves can stay the same for both men and women. The overall structure of the meal prep plan (3 meals, 2 snacks) can likely remain the same. Women typically have lower calorie needs than men due to differences in body size and composition. You might want to adjust the macro targets within each meal. Women often benefit from a slightly higher carb intake compared to men, while protein needs can be similar depending on activity level and goals. Please visit my website's macro calculator to calculate your daily calorie allowance and macro breakdown based on your data and your fitness goal. Then, you can adapt the recipes in this book as explained in the step-by-step instructions above.

Once you have selected a macro split, when should you change it?

It is important to monitor progress and adjust the macros if needed. Aim for 4-6 weeks to assess progress and individual needs. If you are seeing results, there is no need to change the current macro split, at least not immediately. However, even when successful, progress might gradually slow down over time. Minor adjustments (e.g. slightly increasing protein) can help maintain momentum. In case your goal changes (for instance from cutting to bulking) then your macro split will need to change accordingly. If you are not seeing results (muscle gain or fat loss), a change might be necessary after 4-6 weeks. If you hit a **plateau,** then adjusting macros can help break through the plateau. How do you understand if you have hit a plateau? For those aiming for fat loss, weight loss stops or slows down significantly for several weeks. For those aiming for muscle gain, the scale weight doesn't budge, or muscle definition isn't improving. Progress in weightlifting exercises plateaus for several weeks, despite good form and proper technique. You are feeling unusually tired or lethargic despite sufficient sleep and rest.

This can be frustrating, but it's a normal part of the process. Plateau can happen for various reasons.
Metabolic adaptation, your body becomes accustomed to your current calorie intake and exercise routine, making it less efficient at burning calories.
Muscle Memory, as your muscles adapt to training, they may require a new stimulus (increased weight or different exercises) to continue growing.
Nutrient Deficiencies, not getting enough of certain nutrients can hinder progress.
In case you hit a plateau, you should consider the following:

Short-term calorie cycling: For fat loss, slightly reduce calories. A temporary reduction in daily calorie intake (5-10% for a week or two) can force the body to burn more stored fat for energy. For muscle gain, increase calories. A temporary increase in daily calorie intake (5-10% for a week or two) can provide the extra energy needed to break through a muscle-building plateau.

Macro split tweaks: For both goals, increase protein. A slight increase in protein intake (a few percent) can help with muscle repair and growth, even during a cutting phase. For fat loss, consider a low carb day. A strategically placed low-carb day (once a week) can help improve insulin sensitivity and potentially lead to increased fat burning.

Do not make drastic changes: small and controlled adjustments are best to avoid nutrient deficiencies or muscle loss. Remember to track your progress and closely monitor your weight, body composition and performance in the gym. This will help you assess the effectiveness of the adjustments. At the gym try to incorporate new exercises, increase weight lifted, or try a different training program to challenge your muscles in new ways. Keep always in mind it is important to get enough sleep (7-8 hours per night) and stay hydrated drinking plenty of water throughout the day.

Chapter 6: Recipes, Meal Planning and Prepping

I am so excited you have decided to embark into meal prep! This method has literally been life-changing for me. I know you're going to nail it! I wanted to give you a brief explanation of how this works and how to be the most successful with this guide. This guide provides you with 24 delicious and friendly recipes, strategically chosen to offer variety and fuel your fitness goals.

This meal prep system revolves around batch cooking 4 recipes, doubling or tripling each to create a total of 10 lunch and dinner meals for the workweek. Basically, you'll be making enough of each recipe for two or three portions, giving you a stash of prepped meals ready to grab and go. I recommend setting aside 1-2 hours once a week to cook these 4 recipes to cover all your lunches and dinners for the weekdays (Monday to Friday). While you can make more, it can get tiring to manage a larger batch. Four recipes still provide a good variety throughout the week, keeping your taste buds happy and your body energised for those busy workdays. Repeat this process for 4 consecutive weeks, with a new set of 4 recipes each week.

How do I measure my food? Raw or cooked? To ensure accurate portion control, measure all ingredients in their raw state before cooking, unless otherwise specified.

How to complete your daily macros with breakfast and pre/post workout snacks
This meal prep guide focuses on providing delicious and convenient lunch and dinner options to fuel your goals. I have included a few delicious breakfast options – both sweet and savoury – to kickstart your mornings. Remember, these breakfasts will need to be prepared fresh each day and are not included in the Sunday meal prep session. There are a couple of reasons for this:
Firstly, breakfast preferences can vary greatly. Some people thrive on a larger morning meal, while others prefer a lighter option. Additionally, some individuals crave sweet flavours in the morning, while others prefer savoury options. This guide allows you to tailor your mornings according to your individual needs and taste buds. The lunches and dinners provide a solid foundation to hit your daily macronutrient (carbs, protein, fat) targets. You can choose a breakfast that complements your overall macro goals, whether you're a sweet or salty breakfast person. The meal prep plan will provide the macro breakdowns for each lunch and dinner. You can pick one of the breakfast recipes provided or chose another breakfast option. In this case, simply subtract the total macros from your lunch and dinner from your total daily calories and macros based on your goals as explained in chapter 4. This will reveal the remaining macros you have available for breakfast and pre/post workout snacks. With your remaining macros in hand, you can pick a breakfast that fits your needs and preferences. Use online macro calculators or apps to help you calculate the macros in your chosen breakfast ingredients.

Secondly, many athletes and bodybuilders incorporate intermittent fasting (IF) into their routines. By excluding breakfast, you may have the flexibility to implement IF if it suits your preferences. It is important to note that IF is not mandatory for reaching your goals. See the end of the book to download the bonus "How to combine intermittent fasting with weight loss, toning and muscle mass building". Do you prefer to swap meals and eat your planned lunch for breakfast? No problem! The meal prep plans provide options for lunch and dinner, but you can certainly swap one of these meals for breakfast if that better suits your schedule and eating habits. For example, if you enjoy a heartier morning meal, you could choose a lunch option for breakfast, take the planned dinner meal for lunch and skip dinner that day.

This dedicated meal prep plan ensures you have healthy, delicious lunch and dinner meals readily available throughout the workweek. Weekends offer flexibility for social gatherings or trips outdoors. If you plan to extend meal prep to weekends, simply adjust portion sizes and cook proportionally larger quantities, focusing on making extra portions of those meals suitable for freezing.

Dedicate some time once a week to cook all your meals for the week. I normally dedicate Sundays to cook all my meals for the week, you can choose the day that best fits your routine, whether it's Sunday or another day that works for you. This ensures healthy, delicious food is readily available and saves you precious time throughout the week. Get started by checking the weekly meal schedule for lunch and dinner options foreseen. Then, explore the detailed recipes for each dish. Following that, you'll find a comprehensive grocery list for all the ingredients you'll need for the week. Remember to check your pantry first to see what you already have on hand before heading to the shops. Consider buying frozen and pre-chopped veggies if you want to save time however it might be slightly more expensive. Once you have done your grocery shopping, finally dive into the weekly meal prep step-by-step that guide you through cooking all four recipes in just 1-2 hours.

Here's how to organize your prepped meals for optimal storage and freshness:
Fridge storage (up to 3 Days): Meals planned for Monday and Tuesday (including lunches and dinners) can be stored conveniently in the fridge. This ensures they stay fresh and delicious for quick grab-and-go throughout the first couple of days of the week.
Freezer storage (up to 3 Months): Meals planned for Wednesday, Thursday and Friday (including lunches and dinners) can be stored in the freezer. All the food especially the vegetables have been well chosen to ensure a great texture when reheated. The night before consuming the meal remember to defrost the freezer meal for the next day in the fridge. But what if you forget? No worries! Here are some safe methods to defrost a frozen meal:

- **Cold Water Bath:** Submerge the sealed container in a cold-water bath and change the water every 30 minutes. This method can defrost a meal in 1-2 hours depending on the size and thickness. It is recommended to never thaw food at room temperature. This can create a dangerous temperature zone where bacteria can multiply.
- **Microwave Defrost (if container is microwave-safe):** Use the defrost setting on your microwave, following the manufacturer's instructions. Be sure to monitor the food closely and break it up occasionally to ensure even thawing. Cook immediately after defrosting using this method.

Once you have cooked all your meals wait until they have cooled down completely before storing them. This prevents trapped heat and moisture that could lead to spoilage. As explained in chapter 1, use reusable individual containers for storing and transporting meals for grab-and-go convenience. Label all containers clearly with the meal name and date for easy identification. Reheat meals thoroughly using pans or pots, a microwave or an oven.

For a visual reference to all the recipes, check out the bonus section at the end of this book. As a matter of fact, for your ease and convenience I have compiled all the recipes images together into a single file in the bonus section.

Schedule meal prep Week 1

Meal #1 (**Turkey** with veggies and whole wheat pita **wraps**)
Meal #2 (**Salmon** with asparagus, cucumber, cherry tomatoes and **brown rice**)
Meal #3 (Grilled **chicken** skewers with veggies and **brown rice**)
Meal #4 (Classic **roast beef** with crispy roasties)

Weekday	**Lunch**	**Dinner**
Monday	Meal #1 (Turkey with veggies and whole wheat pita wraps)	Meal #2 (Salmon with asparagus, cucumber, cherry tomatoes and brown rice)
Tuesday	Meal #1 (Turkey with veggies and whole wheat pita wraps)	Meal #2 (Salmon with asparagus, cucumber, cherry tomatoes and brown rice)
Wednesday	Meal #3 (Grilled chicken skewers with veggies and brown rice)	Meal #4 (Classic roast beef with crispy roasties)
Thursday	Meal #3 (Grilled chicken skewers with veggies and brown rice)	Meal #4 (Classic roast beef with crispy roasties)
Friday	Meal #3 (Grilled chicken skewers with veggies and brown rice)	Meal #4 (Classic roast beef with crispy roasties)

Grocery list week 1

Pantry items
- Olive oil
- Salt & pepper
- Lemon juice (fresh or bottled)
- Wooden skewers
- 2 large whole wheat pita breads (around 20cm diameter)
- 600g uncooked brown rice

Protein
- 800g lean ground turkey mince
- 3 chicken breasts (boneless, skinless), around 150g each
- 1.35kg Beef Roasting Joint (topside, sirloin, or similar)
- 2 salmon fillets, around 120g each

Vegetables
- 1 medium onion
- 2 red bell peppers (around 100g each)
- 1 yellow bell pepper
- 1 courgette
- 150g broccoli florets
- 1 bunch asparagus spears, approx. 150g
- 1 cucumber
- 50g cherry tomatoes
- 1kg potatoes
- Optional, fresh herbs such as parsley and dill

Turkey with veggies and whole wheat pita wraps

Preparation time: 10 minutes
Cooking time: 10 minutes
Servings: 2
Ingredients:

- 1 tablespoon olive oil
- 1 medium onion, finely chopped (around 100g)
- 1 clove garlic, minced
- 400g lean turkey mince (ground turkey)
- 1 red bell pepper, diced (around 100g)
- 150g broccoli florets, cut into bite-sized pieces
- Salt and freshly ground black pepper to taste
- 2 large whole wheat pitta breads (around 20cm diameter)

Instructions:

1. **Heat the olive oil:** Get a large frying pan nice and hot over medium heat. Add the olive oil and swirl it around to coat the pan.
2. **Soften the onion:** Pop in the chopped onion and cook for 2-3 minutes, or until softened and translucent. Keep an eye on it and give it a stir occasionally so it doesn't catch.
3. **Add the garlic:** Once the onion is softened, add the minced garlic and cook for another minute, stirring frequently, until fragrant.
4. **Brown the mince:** tip in the 400g of turkey mince and break it up with a spoon as it cooks for 4-5 minutes, or until browned all over.
5. **Veggie time:** Add the diced red pepper and broccoli florets to the pan with the browned turkey. Stir-fry for another 4-5 minutes, or until the vegetables are tender-crisp. Broccoli cooks quickly so adjust the timing based on your desired texture.
6. **Season to perfection:** Give the mixture a taste and season with salt and freshly ground black pepper to your liking.
7. **Warm your pitta breads:** warm your whole wheat pitta breads in the toaster or oven for a minute or two, until nice and soft.
8. **Divide the hot turkey mixture** between the two warmed pitta breads.
9. **Store in two separate airtight containers** and store in the fridge for Monday and Tuesday's lunch.
    Per single serving: Calories: 475kcal; Carbs: 30g; Protein: 53g; Fats 19.5g; Sugar: 13g

Salmon with asparagus, cucumber, cherry tomatoes and brown rice

Preparation time: 15 minutes
Cooking time: 20 minutes
Servings: 2
Ingredients:

- 1 tablespoon olive oil
- 2 salmon fillets (around 120g each)
- 1 bunch asparagus spears (approx. 150g)
- 75g cooked brown rice
- ½ red onion, finely chopped
- 1 cucumber, diced
- 50g cherry tomatoes, halved
- Juice of ½ lemon
- Salt and freshly ground black pepper, to taste
- Fresh herbs such as parsley (optional)

Instructions:

1. **Preheat the oven:** Get your oven nice and hot at 200°C (400°F). Line a baking tray with baking paper.
2. **Prepare the salmon:** Place the salmon fillets on the prepared baking tray. Season them generously with salt, pepper, and a drizzle of olive oil. Squeeze some fresh lemon juice over the top.
3. **Asparagus time:** Trim the woody ends of the asparagus spears. Arrange them around the salmon fillets on the baking tray. Drizzle with a little olive oil (consider adding a touch more) and season with salt and pepper.
4. **Bake it up:** Pop the tray into the preheated oven for 10-12 minutes, or until the salmon is cooked through and the asparagus is tender. You can check the salmon is cooked through by gently flaking it with a fork.
5. **Brown rice:** While the salmon and asparagus are roasting, cook the 75g of brown rice according to the packet instructions. You want it fluffy and cooked through.
6. **Start mixing:** Grab a large mixing bowl and combine the cooked brown rice, chopped red onion, diced cucumber and cherry tomatoes. Before consuming, season with a pinch of salt, pepper and a squeeze of lemon juice. Give it all a good mix.
7. **Take out the salmon:** Once the salmon and asparagus are cooked, take them out of the oven.
8. **Prepare the airtight containers:** Divide the brown rice salad between the 2 containers. Top each container with a roasted salmon fillet and a portion of the roasted asparagus. Store in the fridge for Monday and Tuesday's dinner.

    Fresh Touch (Optional): If you have some fresh herbs like parsley or dill, chop them up and sprinkle them over your dish for a touch of freshness.

    Per single serving: Calories: 257kcal; Carbs: 21g; Protein: 30g; Fats 12.6g; Sugar: 5-7g

Grilled chicken skewers with veggies and brown rice

Preparation time: 20 minutes
Cooking time: 15 minutes
Servings: 3
Ingredients:

- 3 boneless and skinless chicken breasts (around 150g each)
- 1 red bell pepper, cut into chunks
- 1 yellow pepper, cut into chunks
- 1 courgette, cut into thick slices (approx.1cm)
- 1 red onion, cut into wedges
- 200g uncooked brown rice
- Salt and freshly ground black pepper to taste
- Wooden skewers (optional: soaked in water for 30 mins).

Instructions:

1. **Cook the rice:** Get started by cooking the 200g of brown rice according to the packet instructions. Once cooked, fluff it up with a fork and set it aside to cool completely.
2. **Chicken time:** Cut the chicken breasts into bite-sized chunks.
3. **Skewer assembly:** Thread the chicken chunks, red and yellow pepper pieces, courgette slices, and red onion wedges onto the soaked wooden skewers. Alternate the ingredients for a colourful and visually appealing skewer.
4. **Seasoning up:** In a bowl, drizzle the olive oil over the assembled skewers. Season generously with salt, pepper and a good squeeze of lemon juice.
5. **Get grilling:** Preheat your grill to medium-high heat. Once hot, pop the skewers on the grill and cook for 10-12 minutes, turning them occasionally, until the chicken is cooked through, and the vegetables are tender-crisp with a slight char.
6. **Brown rice:** While the skewers are grilling, prepare the brown rice salad. In a large bowl, combine the cooled brown rice with the remaining lemon juice, salt and pepper. Give it all a good mix.
7. **Assemble and freeze:** Once the skewers are cooked and cooled, divide them along with the brown rice salad equally between your three labelled airtight containers and store them in the freezer for Wednesday, Thursday and Friday lunch.
   Per single serving: Calories: 450kcal; Carbs: 40g; Protein: 30g; Fat 15g; Sugar: 3-4g

Classic roast beef with crispy roasties

Preparation time: 20 minutes
Cooking time: 1 hour 30 minutes
Servings: 3
Ingredients:

- 1.35kg beef roasting joint (topside, sirloin, or similar)
- 1 kg potatoes, peeled and chopped into large chunks
- 2 tablespoons olive oil
- Salt and freshly ground black pepper to taste

Instructions:
1. **Preheat the oven:** Crank up your oven to 180°C (356°F) for 5 mins.
2. **Prep the Beef:** Grab your roasting joint and rub it all over with olive oil. Season generously with salt and pepper. Make sure you get all sides!
3. **Roasting time:** Place the seasoned beef joint in a roasting tin. Pop it into the preheated oven and roast for roughly 1 hour for medium-rare (or until cooked to your preference).
4. **Crispy roasties:** While the beef roasts, get on with the potatoes. Peel off the skin, toss them in a separate roasting tin with olive oil, salt and pepper. Make sure they get a good coating!
5. **Double Duty Oven:** Chuck the potato roasting tin in the oven alongside the beef. Roast for about 45-50 minutes, or until they are golden brown and beautifully crispy.
6. **Resting & Slicing:** Once cooked, take both the beef joint and the potatoes out of the oven. Give the beef a rest for 10-15 minutes before slicing. This allows the juices to redistribute for a more tender and flavourful experience.
7. **Freezer ready:** Transfer each portion into 3 separate airtight containers. Label them with the date and pop them in the freezer.
   Per single serving: Calories: 620kcal; Carbs: 45g; Protein: 30g; Fat 20g; Sugar: 1g

Meal prep step by step instructions week 1

This guide gets you through prepping all 4 recipes for the week within 1-2 hours.

Step 1: Pre-heat the Oven (15 mins)

Crank your oven to 180°C (356°F). This will be needed for both the Classic Roast Beef and the Salmon with Asparagus.

Step 2: Tackle the Roast Beef & Crispy Potatoes (45 mins)

1. **Prep the Beef:** While the oven preheats, grab your beef roasting joint. Rub it all over with olive oil and season generously with salt and pepper. Ensure all sides are coated.
2. **Roasting Time:** Place the seasoned beef joint in a roasting tin. Pop it into the preheated oven. Roast for roughly 1 hour for medium-rare (or adjust for your preference).
3. **Crispy Potato Prep:** While the beef roasts, peel and chop the 1 kg potatoes into large chunks.
4. **Double Duty Oven:** In a separate roasting tin, toss the potato chunks with olive oil, salt, and pepper. Ensure they get a good coating!
5. **Potato Roasting: Here's the key time-saving tip: After 45 minutes** of roasting the beef, carefully take the roasting tin out of the oven. **Carefully add the potato roasting tin alongside the beef.** Roast the potatoes for about 45-50 minutes, or until they are golden brown and beautifully crispy.

Step 3: Multitasking - Turkey Wraps & Salmon (20 mins)

1. **Turkey Wraps - Prep:** While the beef and potatoes roast, get started on the Turkey Wraps. Finely chop the medium onion. Mince the garlic clove.
2. **Salmon Prep:** Pat the salmon fillets dry with paper towels. Season them with salt, pepper and a squeeze of lemon juice (set aside).

Step 4: Brown Rice on the Side (20 mins)

1. **Start the Rice:** In a separate pot, cook the 200g of brown rice according to package instructions for the Chicken Skewers. Aim for fluffy and cooked-through rice.

Step 5: Turkey Wraps & Salmon Cooking (15 mins)

1. **Turkey Wraps - Cooking:** Heat a large frying pan over medium heat with 1 tablespoon olive oil. Add the chopped onion and cook for 2-3 minutes until softened. Add the minced garlic and cook for another minute, stirring frequently.
2. **Turkey Time:** Tip in the 400g of lean ground turkey. Break it up with a spoon as it cooks for 4-5 minutes, ensuring it's browned all over.
3. **Salmon in the Oven:** While the turkey browns, take the salmon fillets out of the fridge. Place them on a baking tray lined with baking paper. Add a drizzle of olive oil and another squeeze of lemon juice. Pop the tray into the oven alongside the roasting beef for 10-12 minutes (depending on thickness).

Step 6: Chicken Skewer Assembly & Veg Prep (15 mins)

1. **Chicken Skewers - Prep:** While the turkey and salmon cook, cut the chicken breasts into bite-sized chunks.
2. **Veggie Prep:** Cut the red and yellow bell pepper, courgette, and red onion into pieces suitable for threading onto skewers (approx. similar size to chicken chunks).

Step 7: Finishing Touches (10 mins)

1. **Turkey Wraps:** Once the turkey is browned, add the diced red bell pepper and broccoli florets to the pan. Stir-fry for another 4-5 minutes until the vegetables are tender-crisp. Season with Salt and freshly ground black pepper to taste.
2. **Assemble Chicken Skewers:** Thread the chicken chunks, peppers, courgette slices, and red onion wedges onto soaked wooden skewers (if using). Alternate the ingredients for visual appeal. Season with salt, pepper, and a squeeze of lemon juice.
3. **Salmon Check:** Check on the salmon in the oven. It should be cooked through and flake easily with a fork. Once cooked, take it out of the oven.

Step 8: Dividing & Storing (10 mins)

1. **Turkey Wraps:** While the salmon and chicken skewers cool slightly, grab two separate airtight containers. Divide the hot turkey mixture between the containers. Store in the fridge for Monday and Tuesday's lunch.
2. **Salmon with Asparagus:** Prepare two separate containers. Divide the cooked brown rice between them. Top each container with a roasted salmon fillet and a portion of the roasted asparagus. Store in the fridge for Monday and Tuesday's dinner.
3. **Chicken Skewers (Optional):** Once the skewers cool slightly, assemble three labelled airtight containers. Divide the grilled chicken skewers and brown rice salad equally between the containers for Wednesday, Thursday, and Friday lunch (freezer optional, see notes).

Total estimated time: This entire process should take approximately 1 hour and 45 minutes to 2 hours.

Schedule meal prep Week 2

Meal #5 (**Pork** meatballs with **quinoa salad**)
Meal #6 (**Beef** and **bean chili**)
Meal #7 (**Roast chicken** with **roasted potatoes**)
Meal #8 (**Salmon,** courgette and **quinoa salad**)

Weekday	Lunch	Dinner
Monday	Meal #5 (Pork meatballs with quinoa salad)	Meal #6 (Beef and bean chili)
Tuesday	Meal #5 (Pork meatballs with quinoa salad)	Meal #6 (Beef and bean chili)
Wednesday	Meal #7 (Roast chicken with roasted potatoes)	Meal #8 (Salmon, courgette and quinoa salad)
Thursday	Meal #7 (Roast chicken with roasted potatoes)	Meal #8 (Salmon, courgette and quinoa salad)
Friday	Meal #7 (Roast chicken with roasted potatoes)	Meal #8 (Salmon, courgette and quinoa salad)

Grocery list week 2

Pantry items including grains:

- 35g breadcrumbs
- 1 egg
- 3 tablespoons olive oil
- 180g quinoa, uncooked
- 2.5ml garlic powder as well as 2 minced cloves garlic
- 2.5ml onion powder
- Salt and freshly ground black pepper to taste
- 1 tablespoon tomato purée (concentrated tomato paste)
- 1 teaspoon chili powder
- ½ teaspoon ground cumin
- 1 can (400g) kidney beans, drained and rinsed
- 400g chopped tomatoes (fresh or canned)
- Fresh parsley (optional, chopped for garnish), dried thyme and dried rosemary

Vegetables:

- 1 cucumber, diced (approx. 75g)
- 1 ½ red bell pepper, diced (approx. 175g)
- 1 yellow bell pepper, diced (approx. 100g)
- 2 medium courgettes (approx. 300g total)
- 1 medium onion, finely chopped (around 100g)
- ¼ red onion, finely chopped (approx. 30g)
- Cherry tomatoes (around 50g), halved
- 1 lemon
- Fresh parsley, chopped for garnish (optional)
- 675g potatoes, peeled and chopped into large chunks
- A handful of cherry tomatoes (around 50g)

Meat & Seafood:

- 500g lean minced pork
- 450g lean minced beef
- 1 whole chicken (approximately 1.5kg)
- 3 salmon fillets (approx. 170g each fillet)

Pork meatballs with quinoa salad

Preparation time: 15 minutes
Cooking time: 20 minutes
Servings: 2
Ingredients:

- 250g lean pork mince
- 35g breadcrumbs
- 1 egg
- 2.5ml garlic powder
- 2.5ml onion powder
- Salt and freshly ground black pepper to taste
- 1 tablespoon olive oil
- 200g cooked quinoa
- ½ cucumber, diced (approx. 75g)
- ½ red bell pepper, diced (approx. 75g)
- ¼ red onion, finely chopped (approx. 30g)
- Handful of cherry tomatoes, halved (around 50g)
- Juice of ½ lemon
- Fresh parsley, chopped (optional)

Instructions:

1. **Preheat the oven:** Crank up your oven to 200°C (400°F) for 5 mins.
2. **Mix the meatballs:** In a large bowl, combine the pork mince, breadcrumbs, egg, garlic powder, onion powder, salt and pepper. Mix well with your hands or a spoon until everything is evenly incorporated.
3. **Shape & brown:** Form the meatball mixture into small balls, roughly 1 tablespoon each. Heat the olive oil in a frying pan over medium heat. Add the meatballs and cook for 8-10 minutes, turning them occasionally, until browned on all sides.
4. **Bake through:** Transfer the browned meatballs to a baking tray lined with baking paper. Bake them in the preheated oven for 10-12 minutes, or until cooked through.
5. **Prepare the salad:** While the meatballs bake, make the quinoa salad. In a separate bowl, combine the cooked quinoa, diced cucumber, diced red bell pepper, chopped red onion and halved cherry tomatoes.
6. **Dress the salad:** Just before eating, add the lemon juice, chopped parsley (if using) and a pinch of salt and pepper to the quinoa salad. Mix everything well to combine.
7. **Serve & enjoy:** Once the meatballs are cooked through, take them out of the oven. Divide the meatballs and quinoa salad between two separate airtight containers and enjoy!
   Per single serving: Calories: 470kcal; Carbs: 42g; Protein: 25g; Fat 20g; Sugar: 4g

Beef and bean chili

Preparation time: 15 minutes
Cooking time: 30 minutes
Servings: 2
Ingredients:

- 225g lean minced beef
- 1 tablespoon olive oil
- ½ onion, chopped (around 75g)
- 1 clove garlic, minced
- 1 yellow bell pepper, diced (approx. 100g)
- 1 can (400g) kidney beans, drained and rinsed
- 400g chopped tomatoes (fresh or canned)
- 1 tablespoon tomato purée (concentrated tomato paste)
- 1 teaspoon chili powder
- ½ teaspoon ground cumin
- Salt and freshly ground black pepper to taste

Instructions:

1. **Heat the oil:** Heat the olive oil in a large pot or Dutch oven over medium heat.
2. **Sauté the Aromatics:** Add the chopped onion and minced garlic to the pot. Cook for 2-3 minutes, stirring occasionally, until softened and fragrant.
3. **Brown the beef:** Add the lean minced beef to the pot. Break it up with a spoon as it cooks for 5-7 minutes, until browned and cooked through.
4. **Add the beans and vegetables:** Stir in the diced bell pepper, drained and rinsed kidney beans, chopped tomatoes, tomato purée, chili powder, ground cumin, salt and pepper.
5. **Simmer and thicken:** Bring the chili to a simmer, then reduce the heat to low. Cover the pot and simmer for about 20 minutes, stirring occasionally.
6. **Adjust consistency:** Taste the chili and adjust seasonings if needed. If the chili is too thick, add a splash of water or beef broth to reach your desired consistency.
7. **Serve & enjoy:** Once the flavours have melded and the chili is cooked through, divide it between two airtight containers.

    Per single serving: Calories: 450kcal; Carbs: 35g; Protein: 30g; Fat 20g; Sugar: 8g

Roast chicken with roasted potatoes

Preparation time: 15 minutes
Cooking time: 1 hour 30 minutes
Servings: 3
Ingredients:

- 1 whole chicken (approximately 1.5kg)1 tablespoon olive oil
- 675g potatoes, peeled and chopped into large chunks
- 3 tablespoons olive oil
- 3 cloves garlic, minced
- 1 teaspoon dried thyme
- 1 teaspoon dried rosemary
- Salt and freshly ground black pepper to taste

Instructions:

1. **Preheat the oven:** Crank your oven to 200°C (400°F).
2. **Prepare the chicken:** Place the whole chicken in a roasting tin. In a small bowl, combine 1 tablespoon olive oil, minced garlic, dried thyme, dried rosemary, salt, and pepper. Rub this mixture all over the chicken to coat it evenly.
3. **Season the roasties:** In a separate large bowl, toss the chopped potatoes with the remaining 2 tablespoons of olive oil. Ensure they get a good coating! Season generously with salt and black pepper.
4. **Roast together:** Arrange the seasoned potato chunks around the chicken in the roasting tin. This maximises oven space and allows the potatoes to roast alongside the chicken.
5. **Cooking time:** Pop the roasting tin into the preheated oven. Roast for 1 hour 30 minutes, or until the chicken is golden brown and cooked through. The potatoes should be crispy on the outside and tender on the inside.
6. **Basting tip (optional):** Baste the chicken with its pan juices halfway through cooking to keep it moist and flavourful.
7. **Resting time:** Once the chicken is cooked through, take the roasting tin out of the oven. Transfer the chicken to a serving plate and let it rest for 10-15 minutes before carving. This allows the juices to redistribute for a more succulent bird.
8. **Serve & enjoy:** Divide the crispy roasties between 3 airtight containers. Enjoy your delicious roast chicken dinner!
   Per single serving: Calories: 550kcal; Carbs: 40g; Protein: 35g; Fat 25g; Sugar: 2g

Salmon, courgette and quinoa salad

Preparation time: 15 minutes
Cooking time: 20 minutes
Servings: 3
Ingredients:

- 180g uncooked quinoa salad
- 3 salmon fillets (around 170g each)
- Olive oil
- Lemon juice
- Minced garlic
- Salt and freshly ground pepper
- Courgettes (around 250g total)
- Fresh parsley (optional, chopped for garnish)

Instructions:

1. **Cook the quinoa:** Prepare the quinoa according to package instructions. Once cooked, fluff it with a fork and set it aside to cool completely.
2. **Preheat the oven:** Crank your oven to 200°C (400°F) for 5 minutes.
3. **Marinate the salmon:** Place the salmon fillets in a single layer on a baking tray lined with baking paper. Drizzle them with olive oil and lemon juice. Season generously with minced garlic, salt and pepper.
4. **Roast the courgettes:** On a separate baking tray, arrange the sliced courgettes. Drizzle them with olive oil and season with salt and pepper.
5. **Roast together:** Pop both baking trays into the preheated oven. Roast for 15-20 minutes, or until the salmon is cooked through (opaque and flaky) and the courgettes are tender with a slightly caramelized look.
6. **Assemble:** In a large mixing bowl, combine the cooled cooked quinoa, roasted courgettes and chopped fresh parsley (if using). Mix everything well to combine the flavours.
7. **Freeze in portions:** Divide the complete salad mixture (quinoa, courgettes & dressing) into three separate freezer-safe airtight containers.

    Per single serving: Calories: 480kcal; Carbs: 45g; Protein: 25g; Fat 20g; Sugar: 5g

Meal prep step by step instructions week 2

1) **Gather ingredients:** Make sure you have all the components for the four recipes listed above. Refer to the grocery list for details.
2) **Wash and chop vegetables:** While prepping your ingredients, preheat your oven to 200°C (400°F) for the roast chicken.

- Wash and dice the cucumber, red bell pepper, and red onion for the pork meatball salad.
- Peel and chop the potatoes for the roast chicken.
- Wash and slice the courgettes (zucchini) for the salmon salad.

Cooking (1 hour 45 minutes - 2 hours):

Step 1: Roast Chicken & Potatoes (1 hour 30 minutes)

1. **Prepare the Chicken:** Pat the chicken dry and place it in a roasting tin. In a small bowl, combine the olive oil, minced garlic, dried thyme, dried rosemary, salt, and pepper. Rub this mixture all over the chicken to coat it evenly.
2. **Season the Potatoes:** Toss the chopped potatoes with the remaining olive oil in a separate bowl. Ensure they are well coated, then season generously with salt and black pepper.
3. **Roast Together:** Arrange the seasoned potatoes around the chicken in the roasting tin. Pop the roasting tin into the preheated oven and roast for 1 hour 30 minutes. (Optional: Baste the chicken with its pan juices halfway through cooking for extra moisture.)
4. **Resting Time:** Once the chicken is golden brown and cooked through (juices run clear when pierced near the thigh), take the roasting tin out of the oven. Transfer the chicken to a serving plate and let it rest for 10-15 minutes before carving. This allows the juices to redistribute for a more flavourful bird.

Step 2: Pork Meatballs with Quinoa Salad (while the chicken roasts - 30 minutes)

1. **Cook the Quinoa:** While the chicken roasts, follow the package instructions to cook the quinoa. Once cooked, fluff it with a fork and set it aside to cool completely.
2. **Mix the Meatballs:** In a large bowl, combine the pork mince, breadcrumbs, egg, garlic powder, onion powder, salt, and pepper. Mix well with your hands or a spoon until everything is evenly incorporated.
3. **Shape & Brown:** Form the meatball mixture into small balls, roughly 1 tablespoon each. Heat the olive oil in a frying pan over medium heat. Add the meatballs and cook for 8-10 minutes, turning them occasionally, until browned on all sides.
4. **Bake Through:** Transfer the browned meatballs to a baking tray lined with baking paper. Bake them in the oven (alongside the chicken for the last 10-12 minutes) or until cooked through.
5. **Prepare the Salad:** While the meatballs bake, combine the cooked quinoa, diced vegetables (cucumber, red bell pepper, red onion) and halved cherry tomatoes in a separate bowl.
6. **Dress the Salad:** Just before serving, add the lemon juice, chopped parsley (if using), and a pinch of salt and pepper to the quinoa salad. Mix everything well to combine.

Step 3: Salmon Courgette & Quinoa Salad (after chicken comes out - 20 minutes)

1. **Assemble the Salmon:** Once the chicken is resting, arrange the salmon fillets in a single layer on a separate baking tray lined with baking paper. Drizzle them with olive oil and lemon juice. Season generously with minced garlic, salt, and pepper.
2. **Roast the Courgettes:** On another baking tray, arrange the sliced courgettes. Drizzle them with olive oil and season with salt and pepper.
3. **Roast Together:** Pop both baking trays with the salmon and courgettes into the preheated oven (which should still be hot from the chicken). Roast for 15-20 minutes, or until the salmon is cooked through (opaque and flaky) and the courgettes are tender with a slightly caramelized look.
4. **Combine the Salad:** In a large mixing bowl, combine the cooled cooked quinoa, roasted courgettes, and chopped fresh parsley (if using). Mix everything well to combine the flavours.

Step 4: Finishing Touches (15 minutes):

1. **Carve the Chicken:** Once the chicken has rested, carve it into portions and divide them between two separate airtight containers.
2. **Portion the Salads:** Divide the pork meatball salad and the salmon courgette salad between three separate airtight containers each. This ensures you have three portions of each salad for the week.
3. **Label & Store:** Label all the containers with the contents and date to ensure easy identification during the week. Store them in the refrigerator and enjoy your delicious, prepped meals throughout the week!

Total estimated time: This entire process should take approximately 2 hours.

Schedule meal prep Week 3

Meal #9 (**Tuna and avocado salad** with basmati rice)
Meal #10 (**Chicken** and **veg-stir fry** with noodles)
Meal #11 (**Bangers** and **mashed** potatoes)
Meal #12 (**Beef,** broccoli and **basmati rice**)

Weekday	Lunch	Dinner
Monday	Meal #9 (Tuna and avocado salad with basmati rice)	Meal #10 (Chicken and veg-stir fry with noodles)
Tuesday	Meal #9 (Tuna and avocado salad with basmati rice)	Meal #10 (Chicken and veg-stir fry with noodles)
Wednesday	Meal #11 (Bangers and mashed potatoes)	Meal #12 (Beef, broccoli and basmati rice)
Thursday	Meal #11 (Bangers and mashed potatoes)	Meal #12 (Beef, broccoli and basmati rice
Friday	Meal #11 (Bangers and mashed potatoes)	Meal #12 (Beef, broccoli and basmati rice)

Grocery list week 3

Pantry items including grains

- 180g basmati rice, uncooked
- 125g dried noodles of your choice
- Olive oil
- Salt and freshly ground black pepper to taste
- 2 cloves garlic, minced
- 1 tablespoon soy sauce
- ¾ cup milk
- 3 tablespoons butter
- 1 lemon
- Option 1 (for Beef, Broccoli and Basmati Rice Bowl): 600g fresh chopped tomatoes
- Option 2 (for Beef, Broccoli and Basmati Rice Bowl): 400g canned chopped tomatoes + 1½ tablespoons tomato purée
- Spices: dried oregano, ground cumin, chopped fresh parsley (optional)
- 3 vegetable stock cubes

Vegetables:

- 150g bell peppers, chopped (approx. 75g)
- 75g broccoli florets, chopped
- 50g carrots, chopped
- 25g sugar snap peas
- 1 cup mixed salad leaves (e.g., rocket, spinach, watercress)
- 1 cup cherry tomatoes, halved
- 1 ½ medium onions, finely chopped (approx. 150g)
- 1 whole ripe avocado
- 900g potatoes, peeled and diced
- ¾ teaspoon ground cumin
- Pinch of red pepper flakes (optional)

Meat & Seafood:

- 300g lean minced beef (5%fat or less)
- 2 boneless, skinless chicken breasts (approx. 300g total)
- 9 high-quality pork sausages
- 2 cans (160g total) tuna in brine (drained)

Tuna and avocado salad with Basmati rice

Preparation time: 10 minutes
Cooking time: 20 minutes
Servings: 2
Ingredients:

- 180g Basmati rice (1 cup), uncooked
- 1 can (80g) drained tuna in brine for Monday, 1 can (80g) drained tuna in brine for Tuesday
- 1 whole ripe avocado, diced
- 1 cup mixed salad leaves (e.g., rocket, spinach, watercress)
- 1 cup cherry tomatoes, halved
- 2 tablespoons olive oil
- Juice of 1 lemon
- 1 tablespoon chopped fresh parsley
- Salt and freshly ground black pepper to taste

Instructions:
Sunday:
1. **Cook the rice:** Following the packet instructions, cook the basmati rice. Once cooked, fluff the rice with a fork and spread it on a baking tray to cool completely. This prevents the rice from becoming mushy. Store the rice in two safe separate airtight containers for Monday and Tuesday's lunch.
2. **Prepare other Ingredients:** Dice the avocado, wash and halve the cherry tomatoes and chop the fresh parsley (if using). Store these separately in airtight containers in the refrigerator. Diced avocado stored properly in the fridge can last for 2-3 days at best. Divide the salad, tomatoes, tuna and avocado between two airtight containers for Monday and Tuesday.
3. **Make the Dressing (Optional):** If you prefer to have the dressing ready, whisk together the olive oil, lemon juice, chopped parsley, salt and pepper in a small airtight container. Store it in the fridge for Monday and Tuesday's consumption in the fridge in a separate container.

Monday and Tuesday assembly:
1. **Assemble the salad (both on Monday and Tuesday):** In a large mixing bowl, combine the cooled basmati rice, drained tuna, diced avocado, mixed salad leaves and halved cherry tomatoes.
2. **Dress the Salad (both on Monday and Tuesday):** If you prepared the dressing earlier, toss the salad with just enough dressing to coat the ingredients. Alternatively, you can make a fresh lemon vinaigrette by whisking together olive oil, lemon juice, salt, and pepper in a small bowl. On Monday add only half of the dressing to the salad ingredients and toss gently until everything is well combined, use the residual for Tuesday's lunch.

Per single serving: Calories: 550kcal; Carbs: 40g; Protein: 35g; Fat 25g; Sugar: 5g

Chicken and Veg Stir-Fry with Noodles

Preparation time: 15 minutes
Cooking time: 15 minutes
Servings: 2
Ingredients:

- 2 boneless, skinless chicken breasts, thinly sliced (approx. 300g)
- 2 cups mixed vegetables (150g bell peppers, 75g broccoli, 50g carrots, 25g sugar snap peas) chopped into bite-sized pieces
- 1 tablespoons olive oil
- 2 cloves garlic, minced
- 1 tablespoon soy sauce
- Salt and freshly ground black pepper to taste
- 125g dried noodles of your choice (e.g., egg noodles, rice noodles) cooked according to packet instructions

Instructions:

1. **Cook the noodles:** Bring a large pot of salted water to the boil. Add the dried noodles and cook according to packet instructions. Drain the noodles, rinse under cold water to stop them sticking, and toss with a little sesame oil to prevent them drying out. Set aside in a large bowl.
2. **Prepare the Chicken & Vegetables:** While the noodles are cooking, thinly slice the chicken breasts and chop the mixed vegetables into bite-sized pieces.
3. **Heat the oil:** Heat the olive oil in a large frying pan or wok over medium-high heat.
4. **Stir-fry the Garlic:** Add the minced garlic and cook for 1 minute until fragrant.
5. **Cook the chicken:** Add the thinly sliced chicken breast to the pan. Stir-fry for 5-7 minutes, or until the chicken is cooked through and no longer pink.
6. **Add vegetables:** Add the chopped mixed vegetables to the pan and stir-fry for an additional 5 minutes, or until the vegetables are tender-crisp.
7. **Season and serve:** Season with soy sauce, salt and freshly ground black pepper to taste.
8. **Assemble and Divide:** Divide the cooked noodles between two serving containers. Top each container with half of the stir-fry mixture.
   Per single serving: Calories: 500kcal; Carbs: 51g; Protein: 42g; Fat 20g; Sugar: 5g

Bangers and mashed potatoes

Preparation time: 15 minutes
Cooking time: 30 minutes
Servings: 3
Ingredients:

- 9 high-quality pork sausages
- 900g potatoes, peeled and diced
- 3 tablespoons butter
- ¾ cup milk
- Salt and freshly ground black pepper to taste

Instructions:

1. **Boil the potatoes:** Place the diced potatoes in a large pot and cover with cold water. Bring to a boil over high heat, then reduce heat to medium and simmer for 15-20 minutes, or until the potatoes are fork tender.
2. **Cook the sausages:** While the potatoes are cooking, heat a large frying pan or griddle pan over medium heat. Add the pork sausages and cook, turning occasionally, until browned and cooked through, about 12-15 minutes.
3. **Mash the potatoes:** Once the potatoes are cooked, drain them well and return them to the pot.
4. **Add butter and milk:** Mash the potatoes with a potato masher while adding the butter and milk a little at a time until you reach your desired consistency. Season generously with salt and freshly ground black pepper.
5. **Portion and freeze:** Divide the mashed potatoes and cooked sausages equally between three separate freezer-safe containers (e.g., airtight containers or single-serving portion tubs). Allow to cool completely before placing lids on the containers and freezing.

Per single serving: Calories: 650kcal; Carbs: 55g; Protein: 25g; Fat 35g; Sugar: 5g

Beef, broccoli and basmati rice

Preparation time: 5 minutes
Cooking time: 15-20 minutes
Servings: 3
Ingredients:

- 300g lean minced beef (5% fat or less)
- 1½ tablespoons olive oil
- 1½ medium onions, finely chopped (approx. 150g)
- 1 ½ garlic cloves, minced
- 2 red bell peppers, diced (approx. 150g)
- 225g broccoli florets
- 600g chopped tomatoes (canned or fresh) and 1½ tablespoons tomato purée (optional)
- ¾ teaspoon ground cumin and 1½ teaspoons dried oregano
- 3 vegetable stock cubes (crumbled)
- 187.5g basmati rice, rinsed
- 225ml boiling water
- Chopped fresh parsley and pinch of red pepper flakes (both optional)

Instructions:

1. **Prep and cook the rice:** Rinse the basmati rice under cold running water until the water runs clear. While rinsing, chop the onions, garlic, red peppers, and broccoli florets into bite-sized pieces. In a medium saucepan, combine the rinsed basmati rice, boiling water, and a pinch of salt. Bring to a boil, then reduce heat, cover, and simmer for 12-15 minutes, or until the rice is cooked through and fluffy. Set aside.
2. **Brown the beef:** Heat the olive oil in a large frying pan or wok over medium-high heat. Add the minced beef and cook for 5-7 minutes, breaking it up with a spoon, until browned. Drain any excess fat using a slotted spoon.
3. **Sauté the vegetables:** Add the chopped onions and garlic to the pan with the browned beef. Cook for 2-3 minutes, or until softened and fragrant.
4. **Flavour fiesta:** Stir in the diced red peppers and broccoli florets. Cook for another 3-4 minutes, or until the vegetables are slightly tender-crisp.
5. **Tomatoes and spices:** Add the chopped tomatoes, tomato purée (if using), oregano, cumin, and red pepper flakes (if using) to the pan. Stir well to combine.
6. **Simmer and season:** Crumble the vegetable stock cubes into the pan and stir to dissolve. Season with salt and pepper to taste. Bring to a simmer, then reduce heat and cook for 5-7 minutes, or until the sauce thickens slightly.
7. **Assemble for freezing:** Divide the cooked basmati rice equally among three separate freezer-safe containers. Top each container with the flavourful beef and vegetable mixture. Allow to cool completely before placing lids on the containers. Freeze for up to 3 months.

Per single serving: Calories: 450kcal; Carbs: 42g; Protein: 30g; Fat 15g; Sugar: 5g

Meal prep step by step instructions week 3

Preparation (15 minutes):

1. **Wash and chop vegetables:** While the oven preheats (if making Bangers and Mashed Potatoes), wash and chop vegetables for all recipes:
   - Bell peppers (150g) - dice for Chicken Stir-Fry & Beef Bowl
   - Broccoli florets (225g) - chop into bite-sized pieces for Chicken Stir-Fry & Beef Bowl
   - Carrots (50g) - dice for Chicken Stir-Fry (optional)
   - Sugar snap peas (25g) - chop for Chicken Stir-Fry (optional)
   - Onions (1 ½ medium) - finely chop for Beef Bowl
   - Garlic cloves (4) - mince (2 for Chicken Stir-Fry & 2 for Beef Bowl)
   - Cherry tomatoes (1 cup) - halve
2. **Cook basmati rice (20 minutes):** Follow packet instructions to cook 187.5g of basmati rice for the Beef Bowl. While the rice cooks, you can prep other ingredients.
3. **Dice avocado and prepare salad ingredients (5 minutes):** Dice the avocado, wash mixed salad leaves, and prepare other salad ingredients (optional parsley) for the Tuna & Avocado Salad.

Cooking (50 minutes):

1. **Chicken Stir-Fry (15 minutes):**
   - While the rice finishes cooking, heat olive oil and stir-fry garlic and chicken (5-7 minutes).
   - Add chopped vegetables and cook for another 5 minutes. (While stir-frying, move on to the next step)
2. **Bangers and Mashed Potatoes (30 minutes):**
   - Preheat oven to desired temperature (according to sausage package instructions).
   - Boil diced potatoes (15-20 minutes) while preheating.
   - Cook sausages in a frying pan (12-15 minutes).
   - Drain potatoes and mash with butter and milk.
3. **Assemble Tuna & Avocado Salad (5 minutes):** Combine cooked rice, drained tuna, diced avocado, and salad ingredients in a bowl. Prepare dressing (optional).

Beef Bowl & Tidying Up (30 minutes):

1. **Brown the Beef (5 minutes):** While the chicken and sausages cook, heat olive oil and brown minced beef in a large pan. Drain excess fat.
2. **Sauté Vegetables and Add Flavourings (5 minutes):** Add chopped onions and garlic to the pan with browned beef and cook for 2-3 minutes. Stir in diced red peppers and broccoli florets, cook for another 3-4 minutes.
3. **Simmer the Sauce (10 minutes):** Add chopped tomatoes (or canned tomatoes and tomato puree), oregano, cumin, and red pepper flakes (optional) to the pan. Simmer for 5-7 minutes, or until the sauce thickens slightly.
4. **Finish Up (5 minutes):**
   - Divide cooked basmati rice (from step 2) into separate containers.
   - Top each container with the beef and vegetable mixture.
   - Clean up used cooking equipment.

   Total estimated time: This entire process should take approximately 1 hour and 15 minutes.

Schedule meal prep Week 4

Meal #13 (**Spicy chicken** with cous cous)
Meal #14 (**Salmon** with veg and whole wheat pasta)
Meal #15 (**Pesto chicken** with roasted broccoli and cauliflower)
Meal #16 (**Vegetarian chickpea,** couscous and spinach curry)

Weekday	Lunch	Dinner
Monday	Meal #13 (Spicy chicken with cous cous)	Meal #14 (Salmon with veg and whole wheat pasta)
Tuesday	Meal #13 (Spicy chicken with cous cous)	Meal #14 (Salmon with veg and whole wheat pasta)
Wednesday	Meal #15 (Pesto chicken with roasted broccoli and cauliflower)	Meal #16 (Vegetarian chickpea, couscous and spinach curry)
Thursday	Meal #15 (Pesto chicken with roasted broccoli and cauliflower)	Meal #16 (Vegetarian chickpea, couscous and spinach curry)
Friday	Meal #15 (Pesto chicken with roasted broccoli and cauliflower)	Meal #16 (Vegetarian chickpea, couscous and spinach curry)

Grocery list week 4

Pantry items including grains

- 225g couscous (medium grain), uncooked
- Olive oil
- Salt and freshly ground black pepper to taste
- 1 tablespoon curry paste (medium heat recommended)
- ½ teaspoon ground turmeric
- 1 teaspoon ground cumin
- 1 teaspoon ground coriander
- ½ teaspoon turmeric powder
- ½ teaspoon paprika
- 1 onion, finely chopped
- 1 tablespoon ginger, grated
- 4 cloves garlic, minced
- 1 x 400g can chickpeas, drained and rinsed
- 1 x 400g can chopped tomatoes
- 3 tablespoons pesto sauce (fresh or shop-bought)
- Juice of ½ lemon
- Fresh coriander (optional), chopped, for garnish

Vegetables:

- 150g cherry tomatoes, halved
- 1 bell pepper (any colour), sliced
- 1 small courgette (zucchini), sliced
- 1 red onion, thinly sliced
- 400g broccoli florets
- 400g cauliflower florets
- 1 onion, finely chopped
- 150g fresh spinach leaves

Meat & Seafood:

- 2 boneless, skinless chicken breasts (approx. 300g total)
- 2 salmon fillets (approx. 120g each)
- 3 boneless, skinless chicken breasts

Spicy chicken with couscous

Preparation time: 15 minutes
Cooking time: 20 minutes
Servings: 2
Ingredients:

- 1 tablespoon curry paste (medium heat recommended)
- ½ teaspoon ground turmeric
- 50ml olive oil
- 2 boneless, skinless chicken breasts (approximately 300g total weight)
- 150g couscous (medium grain)
- 175ml boiling vegetable stock
- Fresh coriander (optional), chopped, for garnish
- Salt and freshly ground black pepper to taste

Instructions:

1. **Marinate the Chicken:** In a bowl, combine the curry paste, turmeric, salt, and olive oil. Mix well to create a smooth marinade. Add the chicken breasts, ensuring they are well coated with the marinade. Cover the bowl and refrigerate for at least 20 minutes, or ideally overnight for deeper flavour.
2. **Cook the couscous:** While the chicken marinates, place the couscous in a heatproof bowl. Pour the boiling vegetable stock over the couscous and cover the bowl with a lid. Let it sit for 5 minutes, or until the couscous has absorbed all the liquid. Fluff the couscous with a fork to separate the grains.
3. **Cook the chicken:** Heat a grill pan or frying pan over medium heat. Add the marinated chicken breasts and cook for 5-6 minutes per side, or until golden brown and cooked through.
4. **Assemble and serve:** Divide the cooked couscous between two safe airtight containers. Top each serving with a cooked chicken breast. Garnish with a sprinkle of chopped fresh coriander (optional) and enjoy!
   Per single serving: Calories: 450kcal; Carbs: 35g; Protein: 30g; Fat 18.5g; Sugar: 4g

Salmon with veg and whole wheat pasta

Preparation time: 15 minutes
Cooking time: 20 minutes
Servings: 2
Ingredients:

- 2 salmon fillets (approximately 120g each)
- 125g whole wheat pasta (dried)
- 1 tablespoon olive oil
- 1 clove garlic, minced
- ½ red onion, thinly sliced
- 1 bell pepper (any colour), sliced
- 1 small courgette (zucchini), sliced
- 150g cherry tomatoes, halved
- Juice of ½ lemon
- Salt and freshly ground black pepper to taste

Instructions:

1. **Cook the pasta:** Bring a large pot of salted water to the boil. Add the dried whole wheat pasta and cook according to packet instructions. Drain the pasta and set it aside.
2. **Prepare the vegetables:** While the pasta cooks, thinly slice the red onion, bell pepper, and courgette (zucchini). Halve the cherry tomatoes.
3. **Bake the salmon:** Preheat your oven to 200°C (400°F). Season the salmon fillets with salt, pepper and a drizzle of olive oil. Place them on a baking tray lined with baking paper. Bake for 12-15 minutes, or until cooked through and the flesh flakes easily with a fork.
4. **Sauté the Vegetables:** While the salmon bakes, heat the olive oil in a large frying pan over medium heat. Add the minced garlic and sliced red onion and sauté for 2-3 minutes until softened and fragrant.
5. **Add Remaining Vegetables:** Add the sliced bell pepper, courgette (zucchini), and halved cherry tomatoes to the pan. Cook for an additional 5-7 minutes, or until the vegetables are tender-crisp.
6. **Flavour and Combine:** Season the vegetables with salt, pepper, and a squeeze of lemon juice. Add the cooked whole wheat pasta to the pan with the vegetables and toss everything together until well combined and heated through.
7. **Assemble and Serve:** Divide the pasta and vegetable mixture between two serving containers. Top each container with a cooked salmon fillet.
   Per single serving: Calories: 450kcal; Carbs: 35g; Protein: 30g; Fat 18.5g; Sugar: 4g

Pesto chicken with roasted broccoli and cauliflower

Preparation time: 15 minutes
Cooking time: 30 minutes
Servings: 3
Ingredients:

- 3 chicken breasts (boneless, skinless), approximately 150g each
- 3 tablespoons pesto sauce (fresh or shop-bought)
- 400g broccoli florets, cut into bite-sized pieces
- 400g cauliflower florets, cut into bite-sized pieces
- ½ red onion, thinly sliced
- 2 tablespoons olive oil
- Salt and freshly ground black pepper to taste

Instructions:

1. **Preheat the oven:** Preheat your oven to 200°C (400°F).
2. **Prepare the chicken:** Place the chicken breasts in a large baking dish or on a baking tray lined with baking paper.
3. **Coat with pesto:** Spread 1 tablespoon of pesto sauce over each chicken breast, ensuring they're evenly coated.
4. **Roast the Vegetables:** In a separate bowl, toss the broccoli and cauliflower florets with olive oil, salt and pepper. Arrange the seasoned vegetables around the chicken breasts in the baking dish or on the baking tray.
5. **Bake everything:** Bake in the preheated oven for 25-30 minutes, or until the chicken is cooked through (no pink flesh remaining) and the vegetables are tender-crisp.
6. **Cool and portion:** Once cooked, remove the chicken and vegetables from the oven and let them cool slightly. Divide the pesto chicken and roasted vegetables into three equal portions. Allow the portions to cool completely before transferring them into separate freezer-safe containers. Label the containers with the contents and date for easy identification.

   Per single serving: Calories: 450kcal; Carbs: 35g; Protein: 30g; Fat 25g; Sugar: 5g

Vegetarian chickpea, couscous and spinach curry

Preparation time: 15 minutes
Cooking time: 25 minutes
Servings: 3
Ingredients:

- 1 x 400g can chickpeas, drained and rinsed
- 1 x 400g can chopped tomatoes (including juice)
- 150g fresh spinach leaves
- 75g couscous (medium grain)
- 1 onion, finely chopped
- 1 tablespoon ginger, grated (fresh or ground)
- 1 teaspoon ground cumin
- 1 teaspoon ground coriander
- ½ teaspoon turmeric powder
- ½ teaspoon paprika
- 2 cloves garlic, minced
- 1 tablespoon olive oil

Instructions:

1. **Heat the oil and sauté aromatics:** Heat the olive oil in a large frying pan or pan over medium heat. Add the chopped onion, minced garlic, and grated ginger. Sauté for 2-3 minutes, or until the onion is softened and translucent.
2. **Add spices and chickpeas:** Stir in the ground cumin, coriander, turmeric powder, paprika, and a pinch of cayenne pepper (optional). Cook for an additional minute, allowing the spices to release their fragrance. Add the drained and rinsed chickpeas and stir to coat them in the spice mixture.
3. **Simmer with tomatoes and wilt the spinach:** Pour in the chopped tomatoes with their juices. Bring the mixture to a simmer and cook for 5 minutes. Add the fresh spinach leaves to the pan. Stir until the spinach wilts and reduces in volume.
4. **Season and simmer further:** Season the curry with salt and freshly ground black pepper to taste. Simmer for an additional 5-7 minutes, stirring occasionally, until the flavours meld together and the sauce thickens slightly.
5. **Cook the couscous:** While the curry simmers, prepare the couscous according to package instructions. Once cooked, fluff it with a fork.
6. **Portion and freeze:** Allow the curry and cooked couscous to cool completely. Divide the curry into three equal portions and spoon them into separate freezer-safe containers. Top each container with a portion of cooked couscous. Label the containers with the contents and date.
Per single serving: Calories: 420kcal; Carbs: 40g; Protein: 25g; Fat 15g; Sugar: 8g

Meal prep step by step instructions week 4

Preparation (20 minutes):

1. **Wash and chop vegetables (10 minutes):**
    - Dice bell peppers (150g) - for Chicken Stir-Fry & Beef Bowl (optional for Chicken)
    - Roughly chop broccoli florets (225g) - for Chicken Stir-Fry & Beef Bowl
    - Carrots (50g) - dice for Chicken Stir-Fry (optional)
    - Sugar snap peas (25g) - chop for Chicken Stir-Fry (optional)
    - Onions (1 ½ medium) - finely chop for Beef Bowl
    - Garlic cloves (8) - mince (4 for Chicken Stir-Fry & 4 for Beef Bowl)
    - Cherry tomatoes (1 cup) - halve
2. **Cook basmati rice (optional, 20 minutes):** If making the Beef Bowl, follow packet instructions to cook 187.5g of basmati rice. This can be done while prepping other ingredients.
3. **Marinate Chicken (optional, 20 minutes):** For Spicy Chicken with Couscous, combine curry paste, turmeric, salt, and olive oil in a bowl. Add chicken breasts, coat well, cover, and refrigerate (ideally overnight for deeper flavour).

Cooking (85 minutes):

1. **Spicy Chicken with Couscous (25 minutes):** (If chicken wasn't marinated) While rice cooks (if making Beef Bowl), marinate chicken as above (15 minutes). Cook couscous according to package instructions (5 minutes). Heat olive oil in a pan, cook chicken for 5-6 minutes per side (10 minutes). While chicken cooks, fluff couscous with a fork. Serve couscous with cooked chicken.
2. **Salmon with Veg and Whole Wheat Pasta (25 minutes):**
    - Preheat oven to 200°C (400°F). Season salmon with salt, pepper, and olive oil. Place on a baking tray lined with baking paper and bake for 12-15 minutes (start while chicken cooks).
    - Cook whole wheat pasta according to packet instructions (drain and set aside when salmon goes in the oven).
    - While salmon bakes and pasta cooks, thinly slice red onion, bell pepper, and courgette (zucchini). Halve cherry tomatoes.
    - Heat olive oil in a pan, sauté garlic and red onion for 2-3 minutes. Add remaining vegetables, cook for 5-7 minutes (until salmon is nearly cooked).
    - Season vegetables with salt, pepper, and lemon juice. Add cooked pasta, toss to combine. Serve with baked salmon.

Beef Bowl & Tidying Up (40 minutes):

1. **Brown the Beef (5 minutes):** Heat olive oil in a large pan. Brown minced beef, drain excess fat.
2. **Sauté Vegetables and Add Flavourings (10 minutes):** Add chopped onions and garlic to the pan with browned beef and cook for 2-3 minutes. Stir in diced red peppers and broccoli florets, cook for another 3-4 minutes.

3. **Simmer the Sauce (15 minutes):** Add chopped tomatoes (or canned tomatoes and tomato puree), oregano, cumin, and red pepper flakes (optional) to the pan. Simmer for 5-7 minutes, or until the sauce thickens slightly.
4. **Assemble and Clean Up (10 minutes):**
    - Divide cooked basmati rice (from step 2 or cook now if not making Beef Bowl) into separate containers.
    - Top each container with the beef and vegetable mixture.
    - Clean up used cooking equipment.

Total estimated Time: This entire process should take approximately 1 hour and 45 minutes.

Schedule meal prep Week 5

Meal #17 (**Beef burrito** bowl with brown rice)
Meal #18 (**Feta cheese** and roasted tomato couscous)
Meal #19 (**Lentils** & couscous stuffed bell peppers)
Meal #20 (**Chicken** and brown rice casserole)

Weekday	Lunch	**Dinner**
Monday	Meal #17 (Beef burrito bowl with brown rice)	Meal #18 (Feta cheese and roasted tomato couscous)
Tuesday	Meal #17 (Beef burrito bowl with brown rice)	Meal #18 (Feta cheese and roasted tomato couscous)
Wednesday	Meal #19 (Lentils & couscous stuffed bell peppers)	Meal #20 (Chicken and brown rice casserole)
Thursday	Meal #19 (Lentils & couscous stuffed bell peppers)	Meal #20 (Chicken and brown rice casserole)
Friday	Meal #19 (Lentils & couscous stuffed bell peppers)	Meal #20 (Chicken and brown rice casserole)

Grocery list week 5

Pantry items including grains

- Olive oil
- Salt and freshly ground black pepper to taste
- 200g long grain brown rice (uncooked)
- 250g medium grain couscous
- 150g whole wheat couscous (medium grain)
- 1 x 400g can black beans, drained and rinsed
- 1 jar salsa (medium heat recommended)
- 500ml vegetable stock (enough for 2 servings)
- 1 teaspoon dried mixed herbs (e.g. oregano, thyme, basil)
- 1 teaspoon smoked paprika

Vegetables:

- 2 large onions, finely chopped
- 4 cloves garlic, minced
- 300g cherry tomatoes
- 3 large bell peppers (any colour)
- 1 carrot, grated
- 200g frozen peas
- Fresh parsley (optional, for garnish)

Meat & Seafood:

- 500g lean ground beef (mince)
- 450g chicken breast (boneless, skinless), diced

Beef burrito bowl with brown rice

Preparation time: 10 minutes
Cooking time: 15 minutes
Servings: 2
Ingredients:

- 1 onion, finely chopped
- 300g lean ground beef
- 1 tablespoon olive oil
- 2 garlic cloves, minced
- 1 teaspoon smoked paprika
- 1 x 400g can black beans, drained and rinsed
- 1 jar salsa (medium heat recommended)
- 100g long grain brown rice, cooked (50g per serving)
- Salt and freshly ground black pepper to taste

Instructions:

1. **Heat the oil and sauté: aromatics:** Heat the olive oil in a large frying pan over medium heat. Add the chopped onion and cook for 3-4 minutes, or until softened and translucent. Add the minced garlic and cook for an additional minute until fragrant.
2. **Cook the beef:** Add the ground beef to the pan. Season with smoked paprika, salt, and black pepper. Break up the beef with a spoon as it cooks for 5-7 minutes, or until browned and cooked through.
3. **Add beans and salsa:** Preheat your oven to 200°C (400°F). Season the salmon fillets with salt, pepper and a drizzle of olive oil. Place them on a baking tray lined with baking paper. Bake for 12-15 minutes, or until cooked through and the flesh flakes easily with a fork.
4. **Sauté the Vegetables:** While the salmon bakes, heat the olive oil in a large frying pan over medium heat. Add the minced garlic and sliced red onion and sauté for 2-3 minutes until softened and fragrant.
5. **Add Remaining Vegetables:** Add the sliced bell pepper, courgette (zucchini), and halved cherry tomatoes to the pan. Cook for an additional 5-7 minutes, or until the vegetables are tender-crisp.
6. **Flavour and Combine:** Season the vegetables with salt, pepper, and a squeeze of lemon juice. Add the cooked whole wheat pasta to the pan with the vegetables and toss everything together until well combined and heated through.
7. **Assemble and Serve:** Divide the pasta and vegetable mixture between two airtight containers. Top each container with a cooked salmon fillet.
   Per single serving: Calories: 550kcal; Carbs: 45g; Protein: 35g; Fat 25g; Sugar: 5g

Feta cheese and roasted tomato couscous

Preparation time: 10 minutes
Cooking time: 30 minutes
Servings: 2
Ingredients:

- 150g feta cheese, crumbled
- 300g cherry tomatoes
- 1 teaspoon dried mixed herbs (e.g. oregano, thyme, basil)
- 1 tablespoon olive oil
- 125g couscous (medium grain)
- 1 teaspoon smoked paprika
- 250ml boiling vegetable stock
- Fresh parsley (optional)

Instructions:
1. **Roast the Tomatoes and Feta:** Preheat your oven to 200°C (400°F). In an ovenproof baking dish, combine the crumbled feta cheese and cherry tomatoes. Sprinkle with the mixed herbs and drizzle with olive oil. Toss to coat everything evenly. Roast in the preheated oven for 25-30 minutes, or until the tomatoes are softened and the feta cheese is slightly golden brown.
2. **Cook the couscous:** While the feta and tomatoes roast, place the couscous in a heatproof bowl. Pour the boiling vegetable stock over the couscous and stir well to combine. Cover the bowl tightly with a lid or cling film. Let the couscous stand for 10 minutes, or until the liquid has been absorbed and the couscous is fluffy.
3. **Combine and serve:** Once the tomatoes and feta are roasted, remove them from the oven. With a fork or potato masher, gently mash the feta and tomatoes together in the baking dish, creating a chunky sauce. Fluff the cooked couscous with a fork and then add it to the baking dish with the feta and tomato mixture. Stir gently to combine all the ingredients.
4. **Garnish and Enjoy:** Divide the couscous mixture between two airtight containers. Garnish with chopped fresh parsley (optional) and enjoy.
   Per single serving: Calories: 420kcal; Carbs: 40g; Protein: 25g; Fat 18g; Sugar: 10g

Lentils & couscous stuffed bell peppers

Preparation time: 15 minutes
Cooking time: 40 minutes
Servings: 3
Ingredients:

- 3 large bell peppers (any colour), halved and seeds removed
- 75g whole wheat couscous (medium grain)
- 1 x 400g can lentils, drained and rinsed
- 1 small onion, finely chopped
- 2 cloves garlic, minced
- 1 carrot, grated
- 1 tablespoon olive oil
- 1 teaspoon ground cumin
- 1 teaspoon ground coriander
- ½ teaspoon paprika
- 200ml vegetable stock

Instructions:

1. **Preheat the oven:** Preheat your oven to 200°C (400°F).
2. **Sauté the aromatics:** Heat the olive oil in a large frying pan over medium heat. Add the chopped onion and minced garlic. Cook for 3-4 minutes, or until softened and fragrant.
3. **Add carrot and spices:** Stir in the grated carrot and cook for an additional 2-3 minutes. Add the ground cumin, coriander, paprika, salt, and black pepper. Cook for another minute until the spices are fragrant.
4. **Cook the couscous:** Add the dry whole wheat couscous to the pan and stir to combine with the vegetable mixture.
5. **Simmer with broth:** Pour in the vegetable stock and bring to a simmer. Cover the pan, remove it from the heat, and let it stand for 5 minutes. This allows the couscous to absorb the liquid and become fluffy.
6. **Combine filling:** In a separate bowl, mix the cooked couscous mixture and drained lentils until well combined.
7. **Stuff the peppers:** Place the halved bell peppers in a baking dish. Fill each pepper half with the lentil and couscous mixture, pressing down gently to pack it in.
8. **Bake and brown:** Cover the baking dish with foil and bake in the preheated oven for 25-30 minutes, or until the bell peppers are tender. Remove the foil and bake for an additional 5-10 minutes until the tops are slightly browned.
9. **Cool and freeze:** Allow the stuffed bell peppers to cool completely before transferring them into separate freezer-safe containers. Label the containers with the contents and date.
   Per single serving: Calories: 430kcal; Carbs: 45g; Protein: 25g; Fat 12g; Sugar: 5g

Chicken and brown rice casserole

Preparation time: 15 minutes
Cooking time: 45 minutes
Servings: 3
Ingredients:

- 300g chicken breast (boneless, skinless), diced
- 75g wholegrain brown rice (uncooked)
- 400ml chicken stock
- 1 onion, finely chopped
- 2 cloves garlic, minced
- 100g frozen peas
- 100g diced carrots
- 1 tablespoon olive oil
- 1 teaspoon dried thyme
- 1 teaspoon dried rosemary
- Salt and freshly ground pepper

Instructions:

1. **Preheat the oven:** Preheat your oven to 180°C (350°F).
2. **Brown the chicken:** Heat the olive oil in a large frying pan over medium heat. Add the diced chicken breast and cook for 5-7 minutes, stirring occasionally, until browned on all sides. Remove the chicken from the pan and set it aside.
3. **Sauté the aromatics:** In the same pan, add the finely chopped onion and minced garlic. Sauté for 2-3 minutes, or until the onion is softened and translucent.
4. **Toast the rice:** Add the uncooked wholegrain brown rice to the pan and toast for 1-2 minutes, stirring constantly.
5. **Simmer with broth and herbs:** Pour in the chicken stock, dried thyme, and dried rosemary. Bring the mixture to a simmer.
6. **Add vegetables and chicken:** Add the frozen peas and diced carrots to the pan. Stir to combine. Return the cooked chicken to the pan. Season with salt and freshly ground black pepper to taste.
7. **Bake until cooked:** Transfer the casserole mixture to a baking dish and cover it with foil. Bake in the preheated oven for 35-40 minutes, or until the rice is cooked through and the chicken is tender.
8. **Cool and portion:** Once cooked, remove the casserole from the oven and allow it to cool completely. Divide the casserole mixture into three equal portions. Allow the portions to cool completely before transferring them into separate freezer-safe containers. Label the containers with the contents and date.

Per single serving: Calories: 450kcal; Carbs: 40g; Protein: 30g; Fat 15g; Sugar: 4g

Meal prep step by step instructions week 5

Preparation (30-45 minutes):

1. **Preheat Oven (10 minutes):** While the oven preheats, proceed to the next steps.
2. **Prep Vegetables (10-15 minutes):**
   - Finely chop 2 large onions (1 for Beef Burrito Bowls, 1 for Chicken and Brown Rice Casserole).
   - Mince 8 cloves garlic (2 for Beef Burrito Bowls, 2 for Feta Cheese and Roasted Tomato Couscous, 2 for Chicken and Brown Rice Casserole, 2 for Lentil & Couscous Stuffed Bell Peppers).
   - Grate 1 carrot (for Lentil & Couscous Stuffed Bell Peppers).
   - Dice 200g carrots (for Chicken and Brown Rice Casserole).
   - Halve and deseed 3 bell peppers (any colour) for Lentil & Couscous Stuffed Bell Peppers.
3. **Prep Other Ingredients (10-15 minutes):**
   - Rinse and drain 1 x 400g can black beans for Beef Burrito Bowls.
   - Crumble 150g feta cheese for Feta Cheese and Roasted Tomato Couscous.
   - Rinse and drain 1 x 400g can lentils for Lentil & Couscous Stuffed Bell Peppers.
   - Dice 300g chicken breast (boneless, skinless) for Chicken and Brown Rice Casserole.
   - Measure out dry ingredients:
     - 200g long grain brown rice (uncooked) for Beef Burrito Bowls (cook 100g per serving beforehand).
     - 250g medium grain couscous for Feta Cheese and Roasted Tomato Couscous.
     - 75g whole wheat couscous (medium grain) for Lentil & Couscous Stuffed Bell Peppers.
     - 75g wholegrain brown rice (uncooked) for Chicken and Brown Rice Casserole.

Cooking (60-75 minutes):

1. **Beef Burrito Bowls (15 minutes):**
   - Cook pre-browned rice (100g per serving).
   - Sauté onions and garlic, then cook ground beef with paprika.
   - Add black beans and salsa (heat oven to 200°C/400°F for salmon in next step).
2. **Feta Cheese and Roasted Tomato Couscous (30 minutes):**
   - While beef simmers, combine feta cheese, cherry tomatoes, herbs, and olive oil in a baking dish. Roast in the oven (preheated for Beef Burrito Bowls) for 25-30 minutes.
   - Meanwhile, cook couscous with vegetable stock according to package instructions.
3. **Lentil & Couscous Stuffed Bell Peppers (40 minutes):**
   - Sauté onions and garlic, then add grated carrot and spices.
   - Cook whole wheat couscous with vegetable stock.
   - Combine cooked couscous and lentils.
   - Stuff bell pepper halves and bake in the oven (already hot from Feta Cheese) for 25-30 minutes, then brown for another 5-10 minutes.

4. **Chicken and Brown Rice Casserole (45 minutes):**
   - Brown chicken in a pan.
   - Sauté the remaining +garlic and onions, then toast brown rice.
   - Add chicken stock, herbs, frozen peas, diced carrots, and cooked chicken to the pan.
   - Transfer mixture to a baking dish, cover with foil, and bake in the oven (already hot from previous dishes) for 35-40 minutes.

Finishing Touches (10-15 minutes):

- Divide and store Beef Burrito Bowls with cooked rice, ground beef mixture, and salsa (optional toppings like sour cream and avocado can be added later).
- Mash roasted feta and tomatoes with cooked couscous for Feta Cheese and Roasted Tomato Couscous. Divide and store.
- Allow Lentil & Couscous Stuffed Bell Peppers to cool slightly before storing in containers.
- Once cooked, remove Chicken and Brown Rice Casserole from the oven and allow to cool before dividing and storing in containers.

Total estimated time: This entire process should take approximately 1 hour and 45 minutes to 2 hours.

Schedule meal prep Week 6

Meal #21 (**Prawn**, courgette and rice stir-fry)
Meal #22 (**Cottage cheese,** green beans and quinoa salad)
Meal #23 (**Beef burgers** and sweet potato wedges)
Meal #24 (**Grilled turkey breast** with lemon herb rice)

Weekday	Lunch	Dinner
Monday	Meal #21 (Prawn, courgette and rice stir-fry)	Meal #22 (Cottage cheese, green beans and quinoa salad)
Tuesday	Meal #21 (Prawn, courgette and rice stir-fry)	Meal #22 (Cottage cheese, green beans and quinoa salad)
Wednesday	Meal #23 (Beef burgers and sweet potato wedges)	Meal #24 (Grilled turkey breast with lemon herb rice)
Thursday	Meal #23 (Beef burgers and sweet potato wedges)	Meal #24 (Grilled turkey breast with lemon herb rice)
Friday	Meal #23 (Beef burgers and sweet potato wedges)	Meal #24 (Grilled turkey breast with lemon herb rice)

Grocery list week 6

<u>Pantry items including grains</u>

- Olive oil
- Salt and freshly ground black pepper to taste
- 225g long-grain brown rice (uncooked)
- 250g medium grain couscous
- 150g whole wheat couscous
- 75g cooked rice
- 1 tablespoon Worcestershire sauce (optional)
- 1 tablespoon Dijon mustard (optional)
- 1 teaspoon ginger, grated (fresh or ground)
- 1 tablespoon soy sauce
- 1 tablespoon lemon juice
- 1 tablespoon chopped fresh parsley (optional)
- 150g cottage cheese
- 75g quinoa (uncooked)
- 200ml water
- ½ teaspoon sweet smoked paprika
- ½ teaspoon garlic powder

<u>Vegetables:</u>

- 2 large onions, finely chopped
- 8 cloves garlic, minced
- 1 carrot, grated
- 200g diced carrots
- 300g cherry tomatoes
- 3 large bell peppers (any colour)
- 1 courgette (zucchini), thinly sliced
- 200g green beans, trimmed
- 3 medium sweet potatoes, approx. 450-500g total weight

<u>Meat & Seafood:</u>

- 500g raw prawns, peeled and deveined
- 450g lean minced beef (5% fat or less)
- 450g turkey breast fillet

Prawn, courgette and rice stir-fry

Preparation time: 10 minutes
Cooking time: 20 minutes
Servings: 2
Ingredients:

- 150g raw prawns, peeled and deveined
- 1 courgette (zucchini), thinly sliced
- 75g cooked rice (approximately ½ cup)
- 1 tablespoon olive oil
- 2 cloves garlic, minced
- 1 teaspoon ginger, grated (fresh or ground)
- 1 tablespoon soy sauce
- Salt and freshly ground black pepper
- Fresh parsley (optional)

Instructions:

1. **Heat the oil:** Heat the olive oil in a large frying pan or wok over medium-high heat.
2. **Sauté aromatics:** Add the minced garlic, grated ginger, and chopped red chilli (if using) to the pan. Stir-fry for 1-2 minutes until fragrant.
3. **Cook the courgettes:** Add the thinly sliced courgette to the pan. Stir-fry for 3-4 minutes until the courgette is tender-crisp.
4. **Cook the prawns:** Push the courgette to one side of the pan and add the raw prawns to the other side. Cook the prawns for 2-3 minutes per side, or until they turn pink and opaque throughout.
5. **Combine with rice:** Stir in the cooked rice to the pan, breaking up any clumps. Combine well with the cooked courgette and prawns.
6. **Add Sauce and Stir-Fry:** In a small bowl pour the soy sauce and mix with the shrimp, rice and courgette in the pan. Stir-fry everything together for an additional 2-3 minutes until heated through and evenly coated with the sauce.
7. **Season and Serve:** Season with salt and freshly ground black pepper to taste. Divide the stir-fry mixture into two airtight containers.
   Per single serving: Calories: 380kcal; Carbs: 35g; Protein: 25g; Fat 15g; Sugar: 2g

Cottage cheese, green beans and quinoa salad

Preparation time: 15 minutes
Cooking time: 20 minutes
Servings: 2
Ingredients:

- 75g quinoa (uncooked)
- 200ml water
- 200g green beans, trimmed
- 150g cottage cheese
- 1 tablespoon olive oil
- 1 tablespoon lemon juice
- 1 tablespoon chopped fresh parsley
- Salt and freshly ground black pepper

Instructions:

1. **Cook the quinoa:** Rinse the quinoa thoroughly under cold water in a fine mesh strainer. In a saucepan, combine the rinsed quinoa and water. Bring to a boil, then reduce heat to low, cover the pan, and simmer for 15 minutes, or until the quinoa is cooked through and the water is absorbed. Remove from the heat and let it cool completely.
2. **Blanch the green beans:** While the quinoa cooks, blanch the green beans in a pot of boiling water for 3-4 minutes, or until they are tender-crisp. Drain the beans and rinse them under cold water to stop the cooking process. Allow them to cool slightly, then chop them into bite-sized pieces.
3. **Combine and season:** In a large bowl, combine the cooked quinoa, chopped green beans, cottage cheese, olive oil, lemon juice, and chopped fresh parsley. Season with salt and freshly ground black pepper to taste.
4. **Portion and chili:** Toss everything together until well combined. Divide the salad into two separate airtight containers.
   Per single serving: Calories: 380kcal; Carbs: 35g; Protein: 20g; Fat 18g; Sugar: 3g

Beef burgers and sweet potato wedges

Preparation time: 15 minutes
Cooking time: 40 minutes
Servings: 3
Ingredients:

- 450g lean minced beef (5%fat or less)
- 1 small onion, finely chopped and 2 minced cloves garlic
- 1 teaspoon Worcestershire sauce
- 1 teaspoon Dijon mustard
- Salt and freshly ground black pepper
- 3 medium sweet potatoes, approx. 450-500g total weight
- 1 tablespoon olive oil
- ½ teaspoon sweet smoked paprika
- ½ teaspoon garlic powder

Instructions:

1. **Preheat the oven:** Preheat your oven to 200°C (400°F).
2. **Prepare sweet potato wedges:** Peel the sweet potatoes and cut them into wedges. In a large bowl, toss the wedges with olive oil, paprika, garlic powder, salt, and pepper. Ensure everything is evenly coated.
3. **Bake the wedges:** Spread the sweet potato wedges in a single layer on a baking sheet lined with baking paper. Bake for 25-30 minutes, or until golden brown and crispy.
4. **Prepare the burgers (2 options).**

    Option 1, make your own burgers: While the wedges bake, prepare the beef burgers. In a mixing bowl, combine the lean minced beef, finely chopped onion, minced garlic, Worcestershire sauce (optional), Dijon mustard (optional), salt, and freshly ground black pepper. Mix well with your hands until everything is evenly incorporated. Divide the mixture into 3 equal portions and shape them into burger patties.

    Option 2, Use Pre-Made Burgers: If you're short on time, you can use 3 pre-made beef burgers from the grocery store. Choose lean options with at least 90% beef content. Skip adding Worcestershire sauce, Dijon mustard, salt and pepper in this case, as pre-made burgers are usually seasoned already.

5. **Cook the burgers:** Heat a grill pan or frying pan over medium-high heat. Cook the burger patties (homemade or store-bought) for 4-5 minutes on each side, or until cooked to your desired level of doneness.
6. **Cool and portion:** Once the sweet potato wedges are golden brown and the burgers are cooked through, allow everything to cool completely. Divide the cooked burgers and wedges into 3 equal portions for meal prep. Transfer each portion into separate freezer-safe containers. Label the containers with the contents and date.

    Per single serving: Calories: 550kcal; Carbs: 40g; Protein: 30g; Fat 25g; Sugar: 8g

Grilled turkey breast with lemon herb rice

Preparation time: 10 minutes
Cooking time: 25 minutes
Servings: 3
Ingredients:

- 450g turkey breast fillet, sliced into 3 equal-sized portions
- 50g long-grain brown rice (uncooked)
- 1 tablespoon olive oil
- 1 tablespoon lemon juice
- ½ teaspoon dried thyme
- ½ teaspoon dried oregano
- Salt and freshly ground black pepper

Instructions:

1. **Cook the rice:** In a saucepan, combine the uncooked brown rice with 200ml water or chicken stock. Bring to a boil, then reduce heat to low, cover the pan, and simmer for 25-30 minutes, or until the rice is cooked through and the liquid is absorbed. Fluff the rice with a fork and set it aside.
2. **Prepare the marinade:** In a small bowl, whisk together olive oil, lemon juice, thyme, oregano, salt, and freshly ground black pepper to create a marinade.
3. **Marinate the turkey:** Brush the turkey breast slices generously with the marinade on both sides, ensuring they are well coated.
4. **Grill the turkey:** Preheat your grill or grill pan over medium-high heat. Once hot, place the marinated turkey breast slices on the grill and cook for 5-6 minutes per side, or until cooked through. The internal temperature of the turkey should reach 75°C (165°F).
5. **Portion the meal:** While the turkey grills, divide the cooked brown rice into 3 equal portions for meal prep.
6. **Rest and portion:** Once cooked, remove the turkey from the grill and allow it to rest for a few minutes. Slice the turkey breast, if desired, and divide it with the rice into 3 separate portions for freezing. Allow the portions to cool completely before transferring them into freezer-safe containers. Label the containers with the contents and date.

   Per single serving: Calories: 420kcal; Carbs: 40g; Protein: 40g; Fat 12g; Sugar: 1g

Meal prep step by step instructions week 6

Preparation (30-45 minutes):

1. **Preheat Oven (10 minutes):** While the oven preheats, proceed to the next steps.
2. **Prep Vegetables (10-15 minutes):**
    - Finely chop 1 large onion (for Beef Burrito Bowls). **Reserve the other onion for Chicken & Brown Rice Casserole.**
    - Mince 4 cloves garlic (2 for Beef Burrito Bowls, 2 for Feta Cheese and Roasted Tomato Couscous). **Reserve the other 4 cloves for Lentil & Couscous Stuffed Bell Peppers & Chicken & Brown Rice Casserole.**
    - Grate 1 carrot (for Lentil & Couscous Stuffed Bell Peppers).
    - Dice 200g carrots (for Chicken and Brown Rice Casserole).
    - Halve and deseed 3 bell peppers (any colour) for Lentil & Couscous Stuffed Bell Peppers.
    - Thinly slice 1 courgette (zucchini) (for Prawn, courgette and rice stir-fry).
3. **Prep Other Ingredients (10-15 minutes):**
    - Rinse and drain 1 x 400g can black beans for Beef Burrito Bowls. **Pre-cook 200g long grain brown rice (100g per serving) beforehand.**
    - Crumble 150g feta cheese for Feta Cheese and Roasted Tomato Couscous.
    - Rinse and drain 1 x 400g can lentils for Lentil & Couscous Stuffed Bell Peppers.
    - Dice 300g chicken breast (boneless, skinless) for Chicken and Brown Rice Casserole.
    - Measure out dry ingredients:
        - 75g whole wheat couscous (medium grain) for Lentil & Couscous Stuffed Bell Peppers.
        - 250g medium grain couscous for Feta Cheese and Roasted Tomato Couscous.
        - 75g wholegrain brown rice (uncooked) for Chicken and Brown Rice Casserole.

Cooking (60-75 minutes):

1. **Beef Burrito Bowls (15 minutes):**
    - While the oven preheats (for Feta Cheese & Roasted Tomatoes), heat a pan and cook pre-browned rice (100g per serving).
    - Sauté chopped onions and minced garlic, then cook ground beef with paprika.
    - Add black beans and salsa.
2. **Feta Cheese and Roasted Tomato Couscous (30 minutes):**
    - Combine feta cheese, cherry tomatoes, herbs, and olive oil in a baking dish. Roast in the preheated oven (200°C/400°F) for 25-30 minutes.
    - Meanwhile, cook 250g medium grain couscous with vegetable stock according to package instructions.

3. **Lentil & Couscous Stuffed Bell Peppers (40 minutes):**
    - Sauté the remaining minced garlic (2 cloves) and onions in a pan.
    - Add grated carrot and spices (e.g., cumin, coriander).
    - Cook whole wheat couscous (75g) with vegetable stock.
    - Combine cooked couscous and lentils.
    - Stuff bell pepper halves and bake in the oven (already hot from Feta Cheese) for 25-30 minutes, then brown for another 5-10 minutes.
4. **Chicken and Brown Rice Casserole (45 minutes):**
    - Brown chicken in a pan.
    - Sauté remaining garlic (2 cloves) and onions (reserved for this recipe), then toast brown rice (75g).
    - Add chicken stock, herbs, frozen peas, diced carrots, and cooked chicken to the pan.
    - Transfer mixture to a baking dish, cover with foil, and bake in the oven (already hot from previous dishes) for 35-40 minutes.

Finishing Touches (10-15 minutes):

- Divide and store Beef Burrito Bowls with cooked rice, ground beef mixture, and salsa (optional toppings like sour cream and avocado can be added later).
- Mash roasted feta and tomatoes with cooked couscous for Feta Cheese and Roasted Tomato Couscous. Divide and store.
- Allow Lentil & Couscous Stuffed Bell Peppers to cool slightly before storing in containers.
- Once cooked, remove Chicken and Brown Rice Casserole from the oven and allow to cool before dividing and storing in containers.

Total estimated time: This entire process should take approximately 1 hour and 45 minutes to 2 hours.

Super speedy breakfasts (5 mins max & balanced high protein macros)

Here are 6 breakfast ideas that are all incredibly quick to prepare, hitting that 40/30/30 macro target (approximately) and using readily available ingredients like eggs, yoghurt, fruit and nuts. With these options, you can choose between 3 sweet and 3 savoury breakfasts based on your taste preference and to complement your planned lunch and dinner meals for the day. For example, if avocado is already included in your lunch or dinner prep, you might opt for a different breakfast choice to ensure a wider variety of nutrients throughout the day.

While lunch and dinner meals can be prepped and cooked in advance on Sundays, these breakfasts are designed for quick assembly in the mornings to keep your routine streamlined. However, if you're ever short on time during the week, here are some handy tips to make these breakfasts even faster:

- Pre- boil a batch of eggs on Sundays for recipes that call for hard-boiled eggs. This is a great way to grab and go throughout the week.
- Keep chopped vegetables and fruit prepped in the fridge for even faster assembly.
- Use single-serving yoghurt pots for portion control and convenience.
- To save even more time in the mornings, consider portioning out granola, nuts, and sliced fruit into containers for easy grab-and-go assembly.
- If you're using frozen berries, you don't need to thaw them before adding them to your yoghurt bowl or scrambled eggs – they'll help keep your breakfast cool on a warm morning.
- Consider investing in a good quality frying pan for perfectly cooked scrambled or poached eggs.

Double decker smoky salmon and cottage cheese on rye bread

Preparation time: 1 minute
Cooking time: 3-4 minutes
Servings: 1
Ingredients:

- 150g cottage cheese
- 2 slices rye bread
- 2 slices smoked salmon

Instructions:

1. Spread half of the cottage cheese (75g) on each slice of rye bread (1 min).
2. Top each slice of bread with smoked salmon.
   Per single serving: Calories: 250kcal; Carbs: 30g; Protein: 30g; Fat 10g; Sugar: 6g

Smashed avocado with poached egg on toast

Preparation time: 1 minute
Cooking time: 3-4 minutes
Servings: 1
Ingredients:

- 1 ripe avocado, mashed
- 2 large eggs
- Splash of white vinegar (optional)
- 1 slice whole wheat bread (toasted)
- Salt and freshly ground black pepper to taste

Instructions:

1. Bring a saucepan of water to a simmer. Add a splash of white vinegar (optional) to help the eggs hold their shape.
2. Crack each egg into a small separate bowl.
3. Gently swirl the simmering water to create a vortex and then carefully slide each egg into the centre.
4. Poach the eggs for 3-4 minutes until the whites are set and the yolks are runny (depending on preference).
5. While the eggs are poaching, toast the bread.
6. Mash the avocado and spread on the toasted bread.
7. Season with Salt and freshly ground black pepper to taste.
8. Remove the eggs with a slotted spoon and drain on paper towels.
9. Place the poached eggs on top of the avocado toast.
   Per single serving: Calories: 400kcal; Carbs: 35g; Protein: 18g; Fat 20g; Sugar: 2g

Stovetop scrambled eggs with berries

Preparation time: 1 minute
Cooking time: 2-3 minutes
Servings: 1
Ingredients:

- 2 large eggs
- Splash of milk (optional)
- Handful of berries (fresh or frozen)
- Knob of butter

Instructions:

1. Whisk eggs and milk (optional) in a bowl (1 min).
2. Melt butter in a non-stick pan over medium heat.
3. Pour in the egg mixture and gently stir with a spatula until cooked through to your desired consistency (2-3 mins).
4. Remove from heat and fold in berries.
   Per single serving: Calories: 230kcal; Carbs: 3g; Protein: 12g; Fat 18g; Sugar: 2g

Fruity yoghurt bowl

Preparation time: 1 minute
Cooking time: 0 minutes
Servings: 1
Ingredients:

- 150g Greek yoghurt (whole milk or fat-free)
- ¼ cup berries (fresh or frozen)
- 2 tablespoon chopped nuts granola (almond walnuts)
- 1 tablespoon seeds (chia, flax)

Instructions:

1. In a bowl, combine yoghurt, berries, granola and honey (optional).
Per single serving: Calories: 300kcal; Carbs: 30g; Protein: 15g; Fat 15g; Sugar: 15g

Nut butter and banana on toast

Preparation time: 1 minute
Cooking time: 2 minutes
Servings: 1
Ingredients:

- 2 slices whole wheat bread
- 2 tablespoon nut butter (almond or peanut)
- ½ banana sliced

Instructions:
1. Toast bread.
2. Spread nut butter on toast and top with banana slices.
    Per single serving: Calories: 420kcal; Carbs: 50g; Protein: 16g; Fat 24g; Sugar: 18g

Berry oats with nut butter

Preparation time: 1 minute
Cooking time: 1-2 minutes
Servings: 1
Ingredients:

- 30g rolled oats (quick oats work best for this recipe)
- 120ml unsweetened almond milk (or your preferred milk)
- ½ small banana, sliced
- 1 tablespoon nut butter (almond, peanut, or cashew)
- Handful of frozen berries (approx. 30g)
- Pinch of cinnamon (optional)

Instructions:

1. In a microwave-safe bowl, combine rolled oats and milk. If you don't have a microwave, you can cook the oats on the stovetop following package instructions.
2. Microwave on high for 1-2 minutes, or until oats are softened and cooked through. Stir halfway during cooking.
3. While the oats are cooking, slice the banana.
4. Once cooked, take the oats out of the microwave and stir in the nut butter, cinnamon (if using), and sliced banana.
5. Top with frozen berries.
   Per single serving: Calories: 310kcal; Carbs: 42g; Protein: 12g; Fat 14g; Sugar: 7g

BONUS

HERE IS YOUR FREE BONUS!

I would like to take this opportunity to thank you for purchasing "The Complete High-Protein Meal Prep Guide & Cookbook" and to offer you few bonuses. These resources will complement your meal prep journey with valuable resources.

Your support means a lot to me and would be incredibly helpful in promoting awareness about my endeavours. If you enjoy this cookbook, please consider leaving a review on Amazon, thank you!

These are the bonus available for you:

1. Body measurement tracker
2. Carb cycling
3. How to combine intermittent fasting with weight loss, toning and muscle mass building

Don't forget to check out my website for all Recipes' Visualisations.

Please visit my website to download the bonus content:
www.fitnessmealprep.com/Extra/Bonus.html

Conversion Table

Volume Measurements

UK measurement	USA measurement
1 millilitre (ml)	1 millilitre (ml)
1 fluid ounce (fl oz)	29.57 millilitres (ml)
1 tablespoon (tbsp)	3 teaspoons (tsp)
1 dessert spoon	2 tablespoons (tbsp)
1 quarter pint (qt pt)	4 fluid ounces (fl oz)
1 pint (pt)	20 fluid ounces (fl oz)
1 litre (l)	33.814 fluid ounces (fl oz)
1 gallon (gal)	4.546 litres (l)
1 cup	236.59 millilitres (ml)

Weight Measurements

UK measurement	USA measurement
1 gram (g)	1 gram (g)
1 ounce (oz)	28.35 grams (g)
1 pound (lb)	453.59 grams (g)
1 stone (st)	6.35 kilograms (kg)

Temperature Measurements, Formula °F = (°C x 9/5) + 32

UK measurement (°C)	USA measurement (°F)
0	32
25	77
100 (boiling)	212
180 (baking)	350
200 (baking)	392

Other Conversions

UK measurement	USA measurement
1 teaspoon (tsp)	5 millilitres (ml)
1 inch (in)	2.54 centimetres (cm)
1 foot (ft)	30.48 centimetres (cm)

Index

Avocado with poached egg on toast, 87
Beef and bean chili, 49
Beef burgers and sweet potato wedges, 81
Beef burrito bowl with brown rice, 71
Beef, broccoli and basmati rice, 59
Beef,roasted,with crispy roasties, 43
Berry oats with nut butter, 91
Chicken and brown rice casserole, 74
Chicken and potatoes roasted, 50
Chicken and Veg Stir-Fry with Noodles, 57
Chicken skewers with veggies,brown rice, 42
Chicken spicy with couscous, 63
Chicken,pesto,with broccoli and cauliflower, 65
Chickpea, couscous and spinach curry, 66
Cottage cheese, green beans and quinoa salad, 80

Eggs scrambled with berries, 88
Feta cheese and roasted tomato couscous, 72
Lentils & couscous stuffed bell peppers, 73
Nut butter and banana on toast, 90
Pork meatballs with quinoa, 48
Pork sausages and mashed potatoes, 58
Prawn, courgette and rice stir-fry, 79
Salmon with veg and whole wheat pasta, 64
Salmon, courgette and quinoa salad, 51
Salmon,asparagus,cucumber,tomatoes,rice, 41
Salmon,smoked,cottage cheese on rye bread, 86
Tuna and avocado salad with rice, 56
Turkey breast with lemon herb rice, 82
Turkey with veggies wraps, 40
Yoghurt fruit bowl, 89

Conclusion

Congratulations on reaching the end of "The Complete High-Protein Meal Prep Guide & Cookbook"! You've taken a significant step towards achieving your goals by equipping yourself with the knowledge and tools for success. Now it's time to put your newfound knowledge into action! Remember, consistency is key. You can repeat the plan for continued success or adapt new recipes to your individual macros. Don't be afraid to personalize the recipes in this book to suit your taste preferences and dietary needs. By incorporating a high-protein meal prep into your routine you will fuel your body for optimal performance, feel empowered by your healthy choices and witness the incredible results of your dedication.

Keep exploring new recipes, experiment with flavours, exercise regularly, track your progress and most importantly enjoy the journey!

Printed in Great Britain
by Amazon